CHRIS ASHWORTH-BENNION

Chris Ashworth-Bennion is an acclaimed writer and playwright from the Vale of Clwyd.

The Red Rogue of Bala is his first professional play.

Josh Azouz
BUGGY BABY & THE MIKVAH PROJECT:
   TWO PLAYS
GIGI & DAR
ONCE UPON A TIME IN NAZI OCCUPIED
   TUNISIA
VICTORIA'S KNICKERS

Mike Bartlett
THE 47TH
ALBION
BULL
GAME
AN INTERVENTION
JUNIPER BLOOD
KING CHARLES III
MIKE BARTLETT PLAYS: TWO
MRS DELGADO
SCANDALTOWN
SNOWFLAKE
UNICORN
VASSA *after* Gorky
WILD

Jez Butterworth
THE FERRYMAN
THE HILLS OF CALIFORNIA
JERUSALEM
JEZ BUTTERWORTH PLAYS: ONE
JEZ BUTTERWORTH PLAYS: TWO
MOJO
THE NIGHT HERON
PARLOUR SONG
THE RIVER
THE WINTERLING

Katherine Chandler
BEFORE IT RAINS
BIRD
LOSE YOURSELF
THICK AS THIEVES

Beth Flintoff
THE BALLAD OF MARIA MARTEN
THE GLOVE THIEF
REBELLIOUS WOMEN

William Gaminara
ACCORDING TO HOYLE
THE NIGHTINGALES
THE THREE LIONS

Alan Harris
FOR ALL I CARE
FOR THE GRACE OF YOU GO I
HOW MY LIGHT IS SPENT
LOVE, LIES AND TAXIDERMY
SUGAR BABY

Matt Hartley
DEPOSIT
EYAM
HERE I BELONG
MICROCOSM
SIXTY FIVE MILES
THE WIFE OF CYNCOED & IDYLL:
   TWO PLAYS

Jennifer Lunn
ES & FLO

Rob Madge
CHARLEY'S AUNT *after* Brandon Thomas
MY SON'S A QUEER (BUT WHAT CAN
   YOU DO?)

Anne Odeke
PRINCESS ESSEX

Azuka Oforka
THE WOMEN OF LLANRUMNEY

Lisa Parry
THE MERTHYR STIGMATIST

Iman Qureshi
THE FUNERAL DIRECTOR
THE MINISTRY OF LESBIAN AFFAIRS

Bea Roberts
AND THEN COME THE NIGHTJARS
IVY TILLER: VICAR'S DAUGHTER,
   SQUIRREL KILLER
THE WHITBY REBELS

Jessica Swale
BLUE STOCKINGS
THE JUNGLE BOOK *after* Kipling
NELL GWYNN
THE PLAYHOUSE APPRENTICE

Jack Thorne
2ND MAY 1997
AFTER LIFE *after* Hirokazu Kore-eda
BUNNY
BURYING YOUR BROTHER IN THE
   PAVEMENT
A CHRISTMAS CAROL *after* Dickens
THE END OF HISTORY…
HOPE
JACK THORNE PLAYS: ONE
JACK THORNE PLAYS: TWO
JUNKYARD
LET THE RIGHT ONE IN
   after John Ajvide Lindqvist
THE MOTIVE AND THE CUE
MYDIDAE
THE SOLID LIFE OF SUGAR WATER
STACY & FANNY AND FAGGOT
WHEN WINSTON WENT TO WAR WITH
   THE WIRELESS
WHEN YOU CURE ME
WOYZECK *after* Büchner

Amanda Whittington
BE MY BABY
THE INVINCIBLES
KISS ME QUICKSTEP
LADIES' DAY
LADIES DOWN UNDER
LADIES UNLEASHED
MIGHTY ATOMS
PLAYER'S ANGELS
SATIN 'N' STEEL
THE THRILL OF LOVE

Chris Ashworth-Bennion

THE RED ROGUE
OF BALA

NICK HERN BOOKS

London

www.nickhernbooks.co.uk

A Nick Hern Book

The Red Rogue of Bala first published in Great Britain as a paperback original in 2025 by Nick Hern Books Limited, The Glasshouse, 49a Goldhawk Road, London W12 8QP

The Red Rogue of Bala copyright © 2025 Chris Ashworth-Bennion

Chris Ashworth-Bennion has asserted his right to be identified as the author of this work

Cover design by Rebecca Pitt

Designed and typeset by Nick Hern Books, London
Printed in Great Britain by Mimeo Ltd, Huntingdon, Cambridgeshire PE29 6XX

A CIP catalogue record for this book is available from the British Library

ISBN 978 1 83904 526 4

Amateur Performing Rights   Applications for performance, including readings and excerpts, by amateurs in the English language throughout the world should be addressed to the Performing Rights Department, Nick Hern Books, The Glasshouse, 49a Goldhawk Road, London W12 8QP, *tel* +44 (0)20 8749 4953, *email* rights@nickhernbooks.co.uk, except as follows:

Australia: ORiGiN Theatrical, *email* enquiries@originmusic.com.au, *web* www.origintheatrical.com.au

New Zealand: Play Bureau, 20 Rua Street, Mangapapa, Gisborne, 4010, *tel* +64 21 258 3998, *email* info@playbureau.com

Professional Performing Rights   Applications for performance by professionals in any medium and in any language throughout the world (including by amateur stock companies in the USA and Canada) should be addressed in the first instance to Nick Hern Books.

No performance of any kind may be given unless a licence has been obtained. Applications should be made before rehearsals begin. Publication of this play does not necessarily indicate its availability for amateur performance.

Woodland
CARBON
www.woodlandcarbon.co.uk
NICK HERN BOOKS
Printed on Carbon Captured paper

www.nickhernbooks.co.uk/environmental-policy

Nick Hern Books' authorised representative in the EU is
Easy Access System Europe – Mustamäe tee 50, 10621 Tallinn, Estonia
email gpsr.requests@easproject.com

For Adam

The Red Rogue of Bala was first performed in the Theatr Weston at Theatr Clwyd, Mold, on 3 November 2025, with the following cast:

FRANCIS JONES-BATEMAN / TOMOS PRITCHARD	Geraint de Carvalho
HELEDD PRITCHARD	Maxine Evans
HERBERT JONES-BATEMAN / GERAINT OWEN	Wyn Bowen Harries
SION PRITCHARD	Julian Lewis Jones
BEATRICE JONES-BATEMAN	Mia Khan
REGINALD JONES-BATEMAN	Qasim Mahmood
COCH BACH Y BALA (JOHN JONES)	Simon Holland Roberts
CONSTABLE EIFION WINSTANLEY	Rhys ap Trefor
JOHN JONES JNR	Theo Woolford

Writer / Awdur	Chris Ashworth-Bennion
Director / Cyfarwyddwr	Dan Jones
Set & Costume Designer / Cynllunydd	Mark Bailey
Songwriter & Musical Director / Ysgrifennydd Caneuon & Cyfarwyddwr Cerddorol	Mared Williams
Lighting Designer / Cynllunydd Goleuo	Simisola Majekodunmi
Composer & Sound Designer / Cyfansoddwr & Cynllunydd Sain	Johnny Edwards
Fight Director / Cyfarwyddwr Ymladd	Bethan Clark
Assistant Director / Cyfarwyddwr Cynorthwyol	Em Dulson
Assistant Designer / Cynllunydd Cynorthwyol	Oliver Harman

Casting Director /	Olivia Barr
Cyfarwyddwr Castio	
Voice Coach / Hyfforddwr Llais	Nia Lynn
Production Manager /	Jim Davis
Rheolwr Cynhyrchu	
Company Stage Manager /	Helen Drew
Rheolwr Llwyfan y Cwmni	
Deputy Stage Manager /	Amy Clarke
Dirprwy Rheolwr Llwyfan	
Assistant Stage Manager /	Vikki Chandler
Rheolwr Llwyfan Cynorthwyol	

Characters

THE LANDOWNERS
HERBERT JONES-BATEMAN, *seventy*
REGINALD JONES-BATEMAN, *nineteen*
FRANCIS JONES-BATEMAN, *ten*
BEATRICE JONES-BATEMAN, *seventeen*

THE VILLAGE
COCH BACH Y BALA/JOHN JONES, *a convict, sixty*
JOHN JONES JNR, *his son, a labourer, nineteen*
CONSTABLE EIFION WINSTANLEY, *a policeman, forties/
    fifti*es
SION PRITCHARD, *the landlord, fifties*
HELEDD PRITCHARD, *the landlady, fifties*
TOMOS PRITCHARD, *their son, fourteen/fifteen*
GERAINT OWEN, *the vicar, eighties*
VILLAGER 1
VILLAGER 2
VILLAGER 3

Setting/Staging

North Wales. Late September/early October, 1913.

All action takes place inside The White Horse inn, Llanfair
Dyffryn Clwyd.

Stage right – door to the outside. Very large, double doors
(outside).

Upstage centre – a long bar, with a cellar trapdoor behind it.

Upstage left – a large fireplace.

Stage left – stairs or a door that lead to the upper floor of the inn
(inside).

Table, chairs, dartboard. Birdcages behind the bar, empty.

The inn is warm, rural, welcoming but poverty seeps out of the cracks in the walls.

Note

John Jones, aka Coch Bach y Bala, was a real person. A notorious but well-loved poacher, thief, jack-of-all-trades, he was famed for his daring prison breaks. On 4 October 1913, John Jones broke out from Ruthin Gaol. On 6 October 1913, he was shot dead by Reginald Jones-Bateman on the Jones-Batemans' land near Eyarth.

Apart from that, everything else within this play is entirely fictional and in no way an attempt to tell the true story or portray the true characters of those involved.

Suggested Doubling

Herbert Jones-Bateman / Geraint Owen
Reginald Jones-Bateman / Villager 1
Francis Jones-Bateman / Tomos Pritchard
Beatrice Jones-Bateman / Villager 2
Constable Eifion Winstanley / Villager 3

Notes on the Text

Where a sentence does not have a full stop, the character is still speaking. They are not interrupted or cut off – more that they have something else lined up to say. But don't get round to saying it.

Where a character prefix is not followed by a line of dialogue – a pregnant pause.

Dialogue in brackets are asides for the benefit of certain characters or for the speaker's own amusement (they are not speaking to the audience).

This text went to press before the end of rehearsals and so may differ slightly from the play as performed.

ACT ONE

The Return of Coch Bach y Bala

September twenty-seventh, ten p.m. Saturday.

The White Horse, Llanfair Dyffryn Clwyd.

COCH BACH Y BALA *stands on a table. He holds a jug of ale in one hand and everyone else in the room in the palm of the other. He is wet and muddy, disheveled but healthy.*

Also in the inn are SION PRITCHARD, HELEDD PRITCHARD, TOMOS PRITCHARD, JOHN JONES JNR, GERAINT OWEN, VILLAGER 1, VILLAGER 2 *and* VILLAGER 3. *All except* GERAINT *crowd round* COCH BACH. GERAINT *sits by the fire, impassive. Asleep?* TOMOS, *only young, is already drunk.*

COCH BACH *is in full flow:*

COCH BACH. But!

I was sold out. (No!)

Yes! A Judas in the midst. A narrow-eyed East Anglian by the name of Frank (*Frank*). Frank had tipped off the prison guards in order to gain an extra dumpling with his stew. And my plan was rumbled.

Seven long years it had taken me to chew through the wall of that cold cell. Seven long years of gnawing like a rabbit. Look at my teeth! They're nothing but stumps.

TOMOS. Look fine to me, Coch.

COCH BACH. Aye, Tom, but *before* they were FANGS. Like Caesar I was lucky enough to be born with a mouth full of wolf's teeth. And good job and all, that wall was two foot thick.

But!

The night I was due to make my escape – through the wall, out through the yard, a quick swim down the Thames before making my way to the Dutch Antilles on a trade ship – *that night* Frank was chewing down on an extra helping of sawdust dumpling with meat and gravy.

I had trusted him, my cellmate of seven years. Many a long night we had spent chewing that wall together. Turns out it meant nothing to him.

He'd sold me out

The game was up (yes, yes, very sad)

Prison guards. Well, they don't take kindly to escaping. They're like that. And old John, well, it was the Hole for him.

Aye, the Hole! You know the Hole, young Tom?

TOMOS. It's. It's a hole, isn't it?

COCH BACH. Well, aye, it is, but let's try and keep a bit of drama here, shall we?

TOMOS. A really
    tiny

COCH BACH. Yes?

TOMOS. dark hole

COCH BACH. Oh!

TOMOS. with teeth

COCH BACH. Ahhh! (That's enough now, Tom Bach.) Tiny? An infant boy wouldn't fit in without folding himself in half. And *dark*? My grandfather was a trapper in the pits in Ruabon when he were a lad, he used to say the dark down there used to stare back at you. Dark so dark you could see your face in it.

Well, the Hole is so dark, a man can see his own soul.

JOHN JNR. And what does your soul look like then, Dad?

COCH BACH. Like me.

But taller. More hair. Jowlier.

Princely.

SION. Ow'd the hell d'you get out the Hole then?

COCH BACH. How indeed.

But they didn't just *put* me in the Hole, no! Not me, not Little Turpin. They knew full well there isn't a prison cell on God's green earth that can keep Coch Bach y Bala. Not even a tiny one.

Not a lock designed by man or God that I couldn't

TOMOS. Chew through

COCH BACH. It has been known. They use very cheap metal sometimes.

No, lad! Stick me in the Hole as I am and the next time you clap eyes on me, I'd have a tan like a Spanish merchant's arse.

So! They cuffed my hands behind my back. And manacled my ankles. And lashed the two together, and bent me over so's I could inspect the soles of my feet. And they fitted a leather mask tight over my face, so's I couldn't see and barely breathe.

Then! (*Then…!*)

Then they took a whole bag of thumb screws and applied one, so tight I could hear my blood squeak, onto each and every finger and thumb, so's I couldn't use them.

Then! They did the same with my toes, cos they knows the Welsh Houdini's got feet like hands, which frightens the ladies but comes in very useful in the bath.

HELEDD. When you take one.

COCH BACH. Then! (Cheeky cow.) They turfed me in the Hole, locking the tiny door with eleven different locks, one for each month of the year they intended to keep me there (having December off for frivolities).

Four of these locks (February, March, July, October, since you ask) were made by King George's locksmith himself. Locks so impenetrable, so intricate, that they can send a man mad just by looking at the key.

Then they bricked up the door, leaving just a tiny hole to slide in food, mainly flat things. And situated a hundred guards – expert marksmen all – with rifles, at the door. Just. In. Case.

It was, as they say

A bit of a pickle.

TOMOS. So how'd you escape from *that*?

COCH BACH. Well, I didn't, I stayed there for three weeks before they got bored of feeding me through a tiny hole, so they let me out. One evening after that they forgot to lock my cell door and I strolled out whilst the guards were at supper.

EVERYONE. Oh!

COCH BACH. Yeah, they used to do it all the time. Could've left any time I wanted, really.

JOHN JNR. Why didn't you, then?

COCH BACH. A man always likes to know where his next meal is coming from.

And besides, the employment market's been terrible. Nothing out there for a man like me.

SION. What, a poacher?

HELEDD. A thief?

COCH BACH. Ahem.

Sailor. Blacksmith. Ironmonger.

SION. Bullshitter.

COCH BACH. Agriculturalist, thank you Siony.

There is shit involved, mind.

And besides. I had my reasons to stay.

TOMOS. Like what?

COCH BACH. *Billy Bingham.*

HELEDD. Billy

COCH BACH. Bingham.

Grizzled old fella. A lifer. No one knew what he was in for. Not even the screws. Not even the JUDGE. When people'd say 'What you in for, Billy?', he'd reply 'Protection'. 'What you need protecting from, Billy Bach?'. 'Not for me' he'd say. 'Not for me.'

So's we can work out from that, he was some kind of nutter and best off in the clink.

SION. What then, you liked his stories did you?

COCH BACH. Some of them. Aye. Some of them.

Especially one.

Took me these last seven years to earn his trust. So's he'd tell me where he'd buried his fortune. His fortune that he oft spoke of.

TOMOS. And?

COCH BACH. And what?

TOMOS. Where is it?

COCH BACH. As if I'd tell you. Anyway, I found it.

HELEDD. What was it?

COCH BACH. Old Billy told me where to look with his dying breath.

SION. Very convenient, that.

COCH BACH. So's after my dip in the Thames, I eschewed the offer of passage to the Dutch Antilles and I hiked for days into the Cotswolds

TOMOS. Where's them?

COCH BACH. Far away, Tom Bach, scary place. Don't worry about it.

There. Turning left at the third cow

JOHN JNR. The third cow in the Cotswolds?

COCH BACH. and pacing out forty yards to the cracked tree. I found Billy's treasure. *Exactly* where he said it was. Disguised as the grave of a royal hound. His *fortune*.

HELEDD. What was it?

COCH BACH. I cleared away the earth and found a chest. A big bloody chest. I heaved this chest out of the ground. And, panting with the effort, I shoved the lid open, the lid heavy as the world.

And, there. There inside. I saw Billy Bingham's 'fortune'. His life's work. This was what Billy called his 'fortune'.

Well, it was a fortune to him. The only thing he loved. The only thing that really made him happy.

TOMOS. Bet it's something shit.

HELEDD. Tomos! Put that ale down.

COCH BACH. Maybe so. But something worth a million pounds, to Billy.

HELEDD. What was it?!

COCH BACH. A million pounds. In gold.

SION. Shut up.

HELEDD. Where is it now then, Coch, your million pounds?

COCH BACH. I used a small amount to buy myself a smart suit and a shiny pair of boots. And I walked to the nearest gambling den and put it all on red.

Lost the lot.

Sort of regret it now.

JOHN JNR. And the suit?

COCH BACH. Played double or quits. Red again. Bloody fix.

    Walked out of there, then straight here, in naught but my undergarments and socks.

SION. How come you're standing there fully clothed then, Coch Bach?

TOMOS. Yeah, where're those clothes from?

COCH BACH. Nicked 'em. From your dad here. Couple of days ago. As I ran through his 'farm'.

SION (*looking at* COCH BACH). He bloody has and all. And what do you mean 'farm'?

HELEDD. Looks nice on you that.

COCH BACH. Fit very well actually.

SION. I'd have more of a farm if it wasn't for that badger.

COCH BACH. What badger?

SEVERAL. No! / Not the badger! / Don't get him on the badger! / Don't bring up the badger!

SION. I'll bring the badger up if I want to, I'll wring its bloody neck.

COCH BACH. Big necks on badgers.

    GERAINT *stands up and makes way to door.*

GERAINT. I'll be off if we're talking about this badger again.

COCH BACH. It's alive! Good evening, Vicar, I assumed they'd had you stuffed and mounted for sentimental reasons.

GERAINT. Will you be bringing hell down upon our heads again, John?

COCH BACH. Could you not stay and give me moral guidance?

GERAINT. God does not get involved in the affairs of men.

HELEDD (*to* VILLAGER 1 *and* VILLAGER 3). Could you two make sure he doesn't end up in a hedge again?

GERAINT, VILLAGER 1 *and* VILLAGER 3 *leave (outside)*.

JOHN JNR. You been here a couple of days?

COCH BACH. Been here a week, boy.

SION. You bugger. My bloody clothes.

COCH BACH. I'm a desperate man, Sion. A convict. If I see a nice pair of knickers on your line as I hurdle your hedge, as I evade the slavering jaws of King George's hounds, well I'll 'ave 'em for a hat.

And if that's a farm, Siony, I'm Lloyd George.

Listen to this!

COCH BACH *brings out a poster and reads from it.*

WANTED: JOHN JONES, ESCAPED CONVICT

S'me.

Aka, The Welsh Houdini. Aka, Little Turpin. Aka, Coch Bach y Bala. Escaped Wandsworth Prison, London, on the evening of twentieth September.

Slight build (cheeky buggers), red hair (yes), pock-marked face (sea-blasted, I think they'll find), short (short!). Last seen wearing Wandsworth Prison overalls (*obviously*).

Oh ho, this is the best bit! Listen to this…

HELEDD. Coch? There's lights coming.

COCH BACH. Aye, could be old Billy, come for his money.

TOMOS. No…

SION (*to* TOMOS). Don't be an idiot.

Best be in the cellar, John.

COCH BACH. Cellar? First place they'd look, Siony.

SION. No one goes in my cellar without my say so. Anyway, it's the only place secure from the outside. Only way in or out is the cellar door here, so off you go.

HELEDD. Hurry up, John. And can the rest of you try and look normal?

Normalish.

TOMOS. How'd you mean?

HELEDD. Drink! Play cards! Make hubbub.

TOMOS. Hubbub?

HELEDD. God give me strength, Tomos Pritchard. TALK.

TOMOS. To who?

HELEDD. My God…

SION. Down you go, Coch. Plenty of beer down there for you. And you'd be used to small dark places, aye?

HELEDD. Ooh we've got some thumb screws and a leather mask somewhere, if you fancy.

COCH BACH. Now you're talking.

SION. Get down there.

COCH BACH. Eh, give us some of that pheasant stew to go down with.

HELEDD. No, that's for the others.

COCH BACH. I bloody caught 'em.

HELEDD. Do you know how many of the village I have to try and feed with those two straggly birds you dragged in? You want Mrs Roberts's boys to go hungry tonight, do you?

COCH BACH. You're a saint, Heledd Pritchard. You should be anointed. Or do I mean beatified? What do I mean?

SION. Down!

COCH BACH *descends into the cellar. The trapdoor is closed. Sion rolls a heavy barrel over the top.*

Everyone spreads out and acts normal. TOMOS *and* JOHN
JNR *move very conspicuously to the dartboard and stand
as if mid-game. They don't play but* TOMOS *stands poised
to throw. Everyone is trying to talk and act normal but are
anxious about who it could be and can't help falling into
silence when...*

HERBERT, REGINALD *and* CONSTABLE WINSTANLEY
enter (from outside), carrying lanterns. Cold, wet.
REGINALD *holds a hunting rifle which he props against the
bar when he enters.*

TOMOS *very deliberately misses the dartboard and tuts
theatrically. Throughout the next few minutes,* TOMOS *will
use the distraction to keep stealing mouthfuls of beer, getting
progressively more drunk.*

HERBERT. Good evening.

REGINALD. Good evening.

HELEDD. Good evening. Good evening, Constable.

WINSTANLEY. Good evening, Heledd.

    Sion.

SION. Good evening.

WINSTANLEY. Tomos.

TOMOS. Evening.

WINSTANLEY. John.

JOHN JNR. Good evening.

WINSTANLEY (*to* VILLAGER 2). And who's this? Is that
    Macsen's youngest?

REGINALD. '*Everyone.*'
    'Good evening, everyone.'
    Carry on, Constable.

WINSTANLEY. Ahem. Certain. 'Clues'. Have come to our
    attention. That is to say, certain 'things' have been, let's say,

discovered. These 'things' or 'clues', evidence I suppose
you'd call it – except it's not 'evidence'

REGINALD. Where is he?

WINSTANLEY. Well well, now hang on a minute

SION. Who's that?

HERBERT. The convict, who else?

REGINALD. John Jones. Where is he?

SION. I don't want to sound impertinent but you're going
to have to narrow it down a bit. There's quite a few John
Joneses round here.

WINSTANLEY. He is right. The only thing we got more of than
John Joneses is Richard Joneses and a lot of them are related
so it can be perplexing.

HELEDD. John Jones the miller, perhaps?

SION. John Jones from Tan y Bryn?

JOHN JNR. John Jones the schoolmaster?

HELEDD. My cousin's a John Jones, perhaps you mean him?

SION. They wouldn't want him love. He's dead.

HELEDD. *That's* right.

WINSTANLEY. One of my officers is John Jones. Though he
does go by 'Jonny'.

TOMOS. Yeah, Jonny Jones.

JOHN JNR. There are four John Joneses in Pwllglas. In the
same family.

HERBERT. Stop playing bloody games.

WINSTANLEY. That's true, that. The *Joneses*. All Johns.

REGINALD. You know damned well who we mean.

WINSTANLEY (*to* JOHN JNR). Hey, and John Jones, you're a
John Jones

HERBERT. The *convict*.

REGINALD. The – what do you call him?

WINSTANLEY. Ah. Coch Bach y Bala. John Jones.

REGINALD. Where is *he*?

SION. Oh, *that* John Jones.

REGINALD. Yes. Do you know where he is?

SION. London. Having a nice stay in prison, I think.

HELEDD. Can I take your coats, gentlemen?

REGINALD. No. Thank you.

HELEDD. You're soaked through.

REGINALD. Thank you. We're not staying long.

Thank you.

SION. Well, sit down at least. Please.

REGINALD. My father might like to.

SION *gestures to Geraint's chair near the fire.* HERBERT *isn't impressed but doesn't resist. He sits.*

HERBERT. Thank you.

HELEDD. Perhaps a drink?

WINSTANLEY. Lovely.

REGINALD. No. Thank you. Your hospitality is very kind but we won't keep you long.

HERBERT. We *know*. He's here.

HELEDD. Where now?

WINSTANLEY. Evidence. Artefacts – not *artefacts*. But things, objects

SION. Artefacts?

WINSTANLEY. Not artefacts

REGINALD. What the constable is trying to say
Is that we have evidence that John Jones has returned to the
area.

HERBERT. Birds. Rabbits. Even sheep.

WINSTANLEY. That's it, *animals*.

REGINALD. Look, there's been more evidence of poaching in
the past few days than there has been in the last four years.
There's evidence too that someone has been dwelling on the
land.

SION. To be honest with you, the last time any of us clapped
eyes on Coch Bach was in the magistrate's court

HELEDD. Oh, now that was something

SION. Three a.m. he finished his speech. He'd have carried on
till daybreak if someone hadn't woken the judge up.

JOHN JNR. Only reason he got sent down is he went on too
bloody long.

SION. Did his own defence, didn't he. Silly bugger. Never did
know when to shut up.

JOHN JNR. Ten years for boring a judge. Bit steep if you ask
me but there we are, I'm not an educated man like you.

REGINALD. Boring a judge?

SION. To tears.

REGINALD. As I heard, it was ten years for a vicious assault.

JOHN JNR. No. That's lies. Rumours spread by

REGINALD. How old was she? Seventy?

JOHN JNR. Seventy-one and it wasn't him.

REGINALD. For the princely sum of – what was it? – five
pounds?

JOHN JNR. He was falsely accused. The police done it before,
pinned any old crime on him to send him down.

SION. John was a thief and an impish fella, alright. But not a thug.

REGINALD. Any old crime? Cracked her skull. Dislocated her jaw. Broke both her wrists

JOHN JNR. He done things but not that. You didn't hear him. If you'd've heard him...

'Five pounds, your honour? Would I, do something like that, like *that*, for five pounds? I am the Welsh Houdini. I could steal the crown jewels, your honour. What would I need with five pounds?'

SION. It's true, you see. Coch only nicked things he didn't need.

To prove a point.

He didn't survive by it. If he had the choice between lifting a purse or an amusingly shaped object of little or no value. Well. You get the idea.

REGINALD. Well, whatever he was in prison for, and frankly I don't care, he's out.

And he's here.

And we think you know where.

(*To* JOHN JNR.) Know where your father is?

JOHN JNR. I was twelve. Wouldn't even recognise him if he walked through the front door right now.

The front door opens. The wind howls. An old man, bent over, swaddled in a ragged cloak, slowly enters (outside). REGINALD *closes the door for him and helps the old man to a chair, which he sits down in slowly and awkwardly – he makes a scene of it.*

COCH BACH. The wind out there could blow the eyelids off a horse.

Everyone in the pub knows it's COCH BACH. WINSTANLEY *suspects something is up but doesn't know for sure.* HERBERT *and* REGINALD *are unaware. The*

locals in the pub react, secretly, in their own way – shock, anger, admiration, joy, fear. Some struggle to conceal their sniggers.

REGINALD. That's it, that's it. There we are. Nasty night. Gosh, you're freezing.

COCH BACH (*looking around*). Oh…

Evening all.

HELEDD. Good evening. Sir.

SION. Hello. You alright there?

COCH BACH. I am just a poor old man. A poor, *hungry* old man. Ignore me. Pretend I am not there. Just a poor, hungry, cold old man, buffeted by the wind, lashed by the rain, barked at by sheep

REGINALD. Good evening. I don't think I – Are you local?

COCH BACH. Me?

REGINALD. Do you all know this gentleman? He is freezing.

HELEDD. Oh yeah. Old… Tim.

SION. Old Tim! Regular he is, Old Tim.

COCH BACH. Evening.

HELEDD. Lives in Ruthin. Must've walked, silly old thing.

REGINALD. That's a hike in this weather. Old Tim.

Reginald Jones-Bateman.

This is my father. Herbert.

You're soaking! He's soaking.

The wind is

We own the land here.

COCH BACH. Well done.

REGINALD. I think Tim could use some supper. I can smell cooking. Hearty, homely… Cooking.

What do you think, Old Tim? I'm happy to buy you supper on a night like this. It's the least we could do.

COCH BACH. Thank you. Now *this* is a gentleman, I can tell. The rest of you...

REGINALD. You are welcome.

You all think that we're

COCH BACH. And ale.

REGINALD. And. Ale. My pleasure.

What have you got on?

HELEDD. Um. Soup.

COCH BACH. Smells like pheasant. To me.

But then I'm a silly old man, thrashed by weather conditions

HERBERT. Pheasant?

HELEDD. Well...

COCH BACH. Pheasant stew. Mmm! I do love a pheasant stew.

WINSTANLEY. Pheasant, eh? And where did you get these pheasants from, Heledd? Sion?

HERBERT. An old friend of yours has been poaching our pheasants. Funny that, isn't it?

COCH BACH. Aye, that'll be it. Heh heh! Someone – heh heh heh! – someone will've poached from *your* land. And – heehee! – flogged 'em to the pub here. Which is also on your land, heh heh!

REGINALD. I see.

SION. We *did*. Buy some pheasants. From a man.

Who was passing through.

Said they were his.

REGINALD. His pheasants?

SION. We had no idea they might have been poached.

REGINALD. Perhaps, Mr Pritchard, you could be a bit more discerning about who you purchase from in the future

HERBERT. Expensive. Aren't they? Pheasants.

WINSTANLEY. Very dear.

SION. He gave us a very good price. I think they were

Going off.

HERBERT. Friend of yours, was he?

WINSTANLEY (*to Reginald*). Mr Jones-Bateman, I have a thought.

Perhaps this man, the one who sold them the pheasants, *was the man we are looking for*. John Jones.

REGINALD. Yes. That's what we're getting at.

WINSTANLEY. Should we ask them?

REGINALD. Why don't *you*?

WINSTANLEY. Ahem. Sion. Heledd. Everyone.

This… gentleman, the one who sold you the pheasants. Was he a small-ish fellow. 'So' high. Slight build. Bright red hair. Pock-marked face. Jaunty gait

HERBERT. Constable Winstanley.

WINSTANLEY. Yes?

HERBERT. Stand down.

WINSTANLEY. Right.

REGINALD. Mrs Pritchard, will you fetch Old Tim a bowl of pheasant stew?

You'll forgive me if I don't reach for my purse. However, I feel I may have already contributed enough to the meal.

And could you bring the rest of the pot to me.

HELEDD. The whole pot?

REGINALD. Yes.

HELEDD. And how would you like me to serve it?

REGINALD. Just please bring me the pot.

    HELEDD *leaves* (*inside*).

    Tim. You are being fed tonight courtesy of, well partially my father and me, but predominantly courtesy of John Jones. Coch...

WINSTANLEY. Coch Bach y Bala.

REGINALD. Bach y Bala.

COCH BACH. No...!

REGINALD. You know him? Very good.

COCH BACH. Young Coch Bach! Young John! Heh heh!

JOHN JNR. Old Tim knows him very well. They go back years.

REGINALD. Good. Perhaps you can help us.

    HELEDD *enters* (*inside*) *with a bowl of stew, which she hands to* COCH BACH.

    Here you are, Tim.

COCH BACH. Ahhh. Pheasant stew. My favourite.

HELEDD. Enjoy.

    HELEDD *leaves again* (*inside*), COCH BACH *eats.*

REGINALD. Whilst you eat, Tim, have a little think about John Jones. Bring him to the front of your mind.

COCH BACH. Aye, aye.

    During the next speech, HELEDD *returns* (*inside*) *with a very large, heavy cooking pot full of stew. Still talking,* REGINALD *takes the pot, opens the front door, and pours the stew into the mud outside. Before finishing his speech, he hands the pot back to* HELEDD, *who takes it away.*

REGINALD. When my father bought Eyarth, we were handed the keys to the Hall, the deeds to the land. And John Jones.

Not physically, he was in Wandsworth Prison four years ago when we arrived from India. But the previous owners made one thing very clear. John Jones was part of the deal. Nothing to be done about him, they said. He was a weed. Not a tree that could be felled, or a river that could be diverted. A weed. That would keep growing and growing no matter how many times you thought you'd finally seen the end of it. Be grateful, they said, that you'll have a period without him. And pray he dies down there.

We thought he would. But he didn't.

And now he's back.

And we've come to / weed the garden.

HERBERT (*cutting him off*). We want the bastard out.

REGINALD. How's the stew?

COCH BACH. Needs more pheasant.

REGINALD. Where's Old Tim's ale? Come on, I thought this place could show some good old-fashioned rural hospitality. This is a thirsty pilgrim!

HELEDD *pours a pint of beer. She hands it to* COCH BACH *when she's done.*

John Jones is in the area. It is *impossible* that someone hasn't seen him, it is impossible that he can hide without detection, therefore *someone*

COCH BACH. Oh ho! They didn't tell you everything about Coch Bach then.

REGINALD. I've heard ALL about John Jones. I've had four years, Tim, of John Jones. Every second sentence out of someone's mouth round here is about John Jones, and he hasn't even been here for seven years. I am well aware of what they say about John Jones.

I joined the *army* to get away from John Jones but they put me in a local regiment and lo and behold everyone there has a tale about him too.

We were in Africa!

Tell me, go on, tell me, any one of you. Tell me something I don't know about John Jones.

Go on.

TOMOS. Bet you don't know he stole a lion from a travelling circus and rode it around like a horse. In Denbigh.

REGINALD. Heard it.

JOHN JNR. He walked from Bangor to Milford Haven in one day. One day!

REGINALD. Yep.

TOMOS. He's escaped from every prison he's been in. Twice some of them.

REGINALD. Yes, well I wouldn't get very far without hearing that one, would I.

JOHN JNR. He stole, brick by brick, the town hall in Bala and rebuilt it in a field near Corwen. And they only noticed when the mayor felt a draft.

REGINALD. Heard that one. Good one.

WINSTANLEY. He did once steal my uniform. By the time I'd caught up with him he'd arrested half the congregation in Llanbedr church, on the grounds their hymns were sung so badly they'd offended our Lord.

REGINALD. And do you hear what you're describing? A thief.

People talk about him as if he's a hero. Like a – a – a – *magician.* Houdini! Houdini hasn't spent half of his life behind bars. Houdini doesn't steal every scrap of food he puts in his mouth. Houdini isn't bloody *Welsh.*

Listen to yourselves. The man's an outlaw. A poacher. A thief. A criminal. A villain. A thug. What else?

Now, tell me, tell me one thing about John Jones that paints a different picture. Because he is, above all, just a man. He's not magic. He's a man.

COCH BACH. He's not a man.

He's a prince.

REGINALD. *Is* he?

COCH BACH. Look.

COCH BACH *reveals two small birds in his cloak. He cups them in his hand. They are silent.*

HELEDD. Bloody hell. Tim.

COCH BACH. Found them down the road. Now listen

These birds stay silent.

Listen

COCH BACH *prods the birds. They are silent.*

And they will only sing when the true ruler of this land bids them to sing.

HERBERT. This is a waste of time.

COCH BACH. You own this land?

Bid them to sing. Go on.

REGINALD. No.

HERBERT. You're as daft as the rest of them.

COCH BACH. Ask them to sing if this is your land. Cos if it is, they will.

Try and make them sing.

TOMOS (*singing, improvising, drunk*). Coch Bach, the leader of the land!

HELEDD. Right, I think it's time for young ones to go to bed.

TOMOS. Oh, no…

HELEDD (*to* VILL2). That means you too. Home. Now.

HELEDD *bundles a resistant* TOMOS *off* (*inside*), VILL2 *leaves* (*outside*).

REGINALD. Constable. Let's move things forward.

COCH BACH. Coch Bach y Bala is the true Prince of Wales.

His lineage goes back. Way back.

Back to Llewelyn and beyond. The birds will sing for him and no one else. The birds will sing for him and then you will know he is the prince of this land.

You can't find him because the land is his and the land hides him. The land protects him. This land is his home.

REGINALD. Constable?

WINSTANLEY. Ahem. We have reason to believe that you are hiding an escaped convict on these premises. Unless you hand over the convict to us, we will have the owner of the premises taken into custody. That is, arrested. That is, you, Sion. Sorry.

SION. Well, hang on a minute. As far as we're aware, John bloody Jones is banged up in Wandsworth Prison. He's seven years into a ten-year stretch. Are you saying he's not in there?

REGINALD. A man famed, *gloried*, throughout the land for breaking out of prison multiple times? YES, we're saying he's not in there, he's bloody escaped.

SION. First we've heard of it.

HELEDD. We've honestly heard nothing of this.

SION. You assume that because there's been a little bit of poaching recently, it's due to a man banged up behind bars three hundred miles away?

HERBERT. Read them the paper.

REGINALD. It's out – Francis has it.

HERBERT. Why the bloody hell has Francis got it?

REGINALD. He wanted to read it.

HERBERT. Useless boy. Get Beatrice to bring it in.

REGINALD *goes to the door*

HELEDD. *Beatrice* is outside? In *this* weather?

HERBERT. Someone had to wait with Francis.

HELEDD. *Francis* is outside? Dear God.

HELEDD *hurries to the door, opens it.*

Good Lord. Get in you two. Come in. Mind the stew.

BEATRICE JONES-BATEMAN, *and* FRANCIS JONES-BATEMAN, *enter* (*outside*). *Both very cold but stoic.*

Get by the fire. Go on.

BEATRICE. Thank you.

HELEDD. I don't want to intrude. But what the hell were you doing making two children stand outside on a night like this whilst you sat by the fire in your coats?

HERBERT. A public house is no place for a young boy. Or a girl.

HELEDD. I think you could have made an exception.

SION. Love…

BEATRICE. We're fine.

HERBERT. The poster, Beatrice. Read it out.

FRANCIS *hands* BEATRICE *a poster.*

BEATRICE. WANTED: JOHN JONES, ESCAPED CONVICT

Aka, The Welsh Houdini. Aka, Little Turpin. Aka, Coch Bach y Bala.

COCH BACH. Aka, the Beast of Bala Lake. Aka, the Scourge of

HERBERT. Quiet, Mad Tim.

BEATRICE. Escaped Wandsworth Prison, London, on the evening of twentieth September.

Slight build

COCH BACH. Nonsense. A giant.

BEATRICE. Red hair

COCH BACH. *Fiery*

BEATRICE. Pock-marked face

COCH BACH. Sea-blasted…

BEATRICE. Short

COCH BACH. A short giant.

BEATRICE. Last seen wearing Wandsworth Prison overalls.

COCH BACH. I bet he looked very handsome.

BEATRICE. If sighted do not approach as he is considered to be dangerous and violent.

COCH BACH. Wouldn't hurt a fly, that man. Not unless that fly had said something very rude or had jostled him.

BEATRICE. For information leading to his arrest, there is a reward of five pounds.

COCH BACH. Very reasonable.

REGINALD. Now. We will give you a night to think it over.

What's the matter? People have done much worse for five pounds.

Constable?

WINSTANLEY. Harbouring a criminal is a very serious crime, folks. You'd all be in trouble if it was found that you were protecting an escaped convict. It's very out of character too, I'll say.

HERBERT. Prison. The lot of you. We won't spare anyone.

REGINALD. Now *we* don't want that. Why should all of you suffer for him?

When we return tomorrow, we would very much like to know the whereabouts of John Jones.

FRANCIS. Why?

HERBERT. Be quiet, Francis.

REGINALD. Tomorrow, Francis, the good people here may be able to tell us where the man that we're looking for is.

FRANCIS. But he's there.

FRANCIS *points to* COCH BACH.

REGINALD. That's

That's Old Tim…

COCH BACH. Old Tim.

FRANCIS. I thought you knew.

COCH BACH. Just a foolish old man, picking pheasant out of his beard

FRANCIS. Did you really steal a town hall?

HERBERT. Eavesdropping, were you?

BEATRICE. I couldn't stop him.

REGINALD. Ah. I see. What a lark.

We've been made fools of. Father, we've been made fools of.

Constable, arrest this man.

WINSTANLEY. Old Tim?

COCH BACH. Just an old man, with naught but his dreams and his socks

REGINALD. It's bloody John Jones!

WINSTANLEY. Oh. Right.

WINSTANLEY *motions towards* COCH BACH *but* COCH

BACH *leaps up, taking off his cloak and putting distance between himself and* WINSTANLEY *and* REGINALD.

John Jones!

During the next exchange he will carefully hand the birds to HELEDD, *who puts them in a cage above the bar.*

COCH BACH. Don't arrest me, Eifion. Please.

Don't do that. You know what happens when you arrest me. I escape.

And that's quite embarrassing for you. Save yourself the trouble. Chum, old pal.

WINSTANLEY. What should I do?

HERBERT. Arrest him!

COCH BACH. *No.*

No, Eifion. This is for the bobbies in London to deal with, not you. I know you dress like a policeman and you say that you are one but I know that you're not really. Not really. You can stick a blue suit on and a funny hat but a policeman's a policeman in his heart. A policeman's the soldier who shoots deserters. That's not you.

Don't ask him to do it, young Reg. He'd never live it down.

REGINALD. Fine.

REGINALD *picks up his hunting rifle and aims it at* COCH BACH.

John Jones I am taking you into custody. I am sure Constable Winstanley wouldn't mind unlocking a cell door for us. Would you?

WINSTANLEY. I could do that.

REGINALD. You're a convict. Refusing arrest. I have every right to *shoot* you. And I will if it comes to it. A landlord has a right to protect his land.

JOHN JNR *stands.*

JOHN JNR. Quite right. Sion?

> SION *comes out and, with* JOHN JNR, *stands in front of*
> COCH BACH.

SION. Right. A landlord has a right to protect his guests too.
My house, my rules.

> I don't want to say you're barred, Mr Jones-Bateman

> But you're getting awful close. We don't have fighting here.

> HELEDD *joins them.* HERBERT *is left behind enemy lines.*
> REGINALD *puts down his gun, fed up.*

COCH BACH. This wasn't my idea. For the record

REGINALD. Bloody hell...

COCH BACH. I was willing to come quietly.

HERBERT. This is an outrage!

COCH BACH. Oh, hello.

> Hey, we've got a hostage!

REGINALD. Don't.

COCH BACH. We could start posting bits of him back to them.

JOHN JNR. In exchange for what?

COCH BACH. A boat.

REGINALD. Father, come over here. They won't stop you.

HERBERT. I bloody well will not. I'm staying by the fire.

> JOHN JNR *tips* HERBERT *back in his chair and drags him*
> *back to* REGINALD.

> Stop that! I said stop it!

SION. Here we are then.

> What now?

REGINALD (*to* WINSTANLEY). Will you be joining them,
Constable?

WINSTANLEY. No, no. I'm the police.

REGINALD. Yes. Yes you are.

You've got till this time tomorrow, Jones.

If you're not gone, and we'll know if you're still here, we will have you arrested. And we will have every one of you here arrested.

It's very simple.

If we see evidence of Jones's existence – ever – we will have you all arrested. Regardless of whether the grand illusionist himself is in custody or not.

If I was you, I'd do the decent thing and turn myself in, Jones.

COCH BACH. If you were me...

REGINALD. Father. Francis. Beatrice. Constable.

Sion, I won't hold this against young Tom. If John Jones is brought in. This won't be a mark against him.

But if you protect John Jones. Then I can't help him.

SION. He's not interested.

REGINALD. He's told me he is.

The army would do him a lot of good.

Good evening.

HELEDD. Good evening.

WINSTANLEY. Goodbye, Sion.

Heledd...

Everyone!

REGINALD, HERBERT, BEATRICE, FRANCIS *and* WINSTANLEY *leave* (*outside*). *During the next few moments,* TOMOS *sneaks down and listens* (*inside*). *He has been listening for some time.*

COCH BACH. I like the new boss. Very stern.

SION. HOW THE HELL DID YOU GET OUT OF THE CELLAR?

COCH BACH. I never reveal my secrets.

SION. If you've chewed a hole in my wall, I'll be furious.

HELEDD (*to* COCH BACH). Why did you do that for, John?

JOHN JNR. It was *brilliant*. The old man looked like he was going to burst.

SION. What the hell do we do now?

JOHN JNR. We stand by Coch.

SION. *Prison*, John. Hard labour.

JOHN JNR. We don't just hand him over or hound him out on their say-so.

SION. What, and I lose the pub? Lose the farm? Our children starve while we stand by your dad?

TOMOS (*to* JOHN JNR). And he said I wouldn't get in the army.

SION. You're not bloody going in the army.

TOMOS. Stay here and starve like you two, I suppose?

SION. There's a farm where there's work to be done.

TOMOS. Hardly.

SION. Well no one's working on anything or going to any bloody army if we're in prison.

JOHN JNR. This is *ridiculous*. You're just going to hand him in?

HELEDD. I don't think we can make your father do anything, John Bach. I think it's up to him.

SION. Well, hang on, I think it's up to us. I know he's your dad

JOHN JNR. My dad? This is Coch Bach! Imagine being known as the people who shopped Coch Bach y Bala? We'd be lynched. No.

SION. I think we should at least talk about it. With Coch. All of us.

TOMOS. Maybe you could go away, Coch. Just for a bit, like.

COCH BACH. That right, Tom?

SION. I'm sure we could come up with a plan. Coch?

COCH BACH. Plan. I've come home, Siony. That's my plan

HELEDD. In the *morning*, we can make a plan, talk, argue, whatever, in the morning. It's late and I hardly think any of you are in a fit state to make decent decisions.

SION. Agreed, love. Come on. Let's at least give Coch one night of peace.

HELEDD (*to* JOHN JNR). That's time then, John.

JOHN JNR (*readying to go*). Dad.

COCH BACH. Aye. Son.

SION. Actually, John Bach, I've got a few crates to shift out back. Mind giving us a hand? Save your old dad a job?

JOHN JNR. Aye.

HELEDD. *Bed*, Tomos.

TOMOS *leaves* (*inside*).

Well, seeing as they know you're here, I'll make a bed up for you Coch. Save you sleeping in a hedge.

John, I'll show you those crates.

HELEDD *leaves,* JOHN JNR *leaves after her* (*inside*), *leaving* SION *and* COCH BACH.

COCH BACH. Drink, Landlord?

Heledd's looking well.

Want to slap me?

SION.

SION *goes to leave. Stops. Returns and hugs* COCH BACH.

COCH BACH. A farmer now, are you?

SION. Trying to survive, Coch. Eh, wait till you see about this badger.

SION *leaves* (*inside*).

COCH BACH *looks around.*

COCH BACH. This badger, eh.

Leaves.

FRANCIS *enters* (*outside*), *carrying two pheasants.*

HELEDD *enters* (*inside*).

HELEDD. Hello.

FRANCIS. Hello.

HELEDD. Are you alright?

FRANCIS. My father wanted you to have these.

HELEDD. Oh right…

FRANCIS. He said he thought you might appreciate an honest supper.

HELEDD. Well. We do. Tell him, thank you.

FRANCIS. I will.

HELEDD. I'll just go put these in the pantry.

Thank you.

FRANCIS. You're welcome.

HELEDD *leaves* (*inside*).

Immediately FRANCIS *goes to the birds in the cage.*

Sing. Sing! Psst. Oi!

They do not sing. He rattles the cage. They make no noise.

Hey. Sing, damn you!

COCH BACH *enters* (*inside*), *peeling an apple with a sharp knife. He eats as they talk.*

COCH BACH. Yes.

FRANCIS. Yes what?

COCH BACH. Yes I really did steal a town hall. A big one.

FRANCIS. How?

COCH BACH. Just took it. It was lying about after all.

FRANCIS. Why would you take a town hall?

COCH BACH. Cos I wanted to.

FRANCIS. Do you just steal anything you want?

COCH BACH. No. I don't steal anything I want.

Except this apple.

FRANCIS. I heard you stole Queen Victoria's bloomers.

COCH BACH. Oh yeah?

FRANCIS. Whilst she was wearing them.

COCH BACH. Sounds like a tall story to me.

Besides. Queen Victoria never wore any bloomers.

FRANCIS. Prince Edward is the Prince of Wales. Not you.
    You're a common thief.

COCH BACH. How dare you. I am a brilliant thief. I am an
    *un*common thief.

FRANCIS. I have seen Houdini and you're nothing like him.

COCH BACH. You're not afraid of me, are you?

FRANCIS. No. Make the birds sing.

COCH BACH. Don't fancy it right now.

FRANCIS. You *can't*! The birds are mute. I know.

I know how Houdini does *all* his tricks. That's all they are,
tricks. There's always a solution.

The birds must be mute. I've worked it out.

COCH BACH. Aren't little boys supposed to believe in magic?

FRANCIS. No.

COCH BACH. What's that around your neck?

FRANCIS. It is a locket. And it is mine.

COCH BACH. Tell you what

I'll steal it. And you won't even notice. How's that for a trick?

Could Houdini steal your locket with your noticing?

FRANCIS. No one could. I never take it off.

COCH BACH. No problem.

FRANCIS. It's impossible. I never take it off. You'd have to force it off me, and then my brother would have you hanged. Which he's probably going to do anyway.

COCH BACH. I said steal. Not force. Deal?

FRANCIS. What do you want in return?

COCH BACH. Well. The locket. Deal?

FRANCIS.

Very well.

I challenge you to steal my locket without me noticing.

You do that and I shall say you are worthy to be Houdini's apprentice.

Deal?

COCH BACH. And when I steal it, I'll have you and your swine family's heads on spikes and I'll parade them through Ruthin, through Bala, through Denbigh, through Mold, through Llangollen and everyone will know that you are dead.

People will line the streets.

FRANCIS. You're a *bastard*.

COCH BACH. I have what is my father's and he had what was his father's before him. You wait till you see what you're left with when the old boy snuffs it. Matey

There are no bastards in Wales.

COCH BACH *leaves* (*inside*).

BEATRICE (*off*). Francis? Francis, what's keeping you?

BEATRICE *enters* (*outside*).

Francis, what have you been doing?

FRANCIS. Nothing.

BEATRICE. Come. We have to get back to Mother.

Who have you been talking to?

FRANCIS. Why won't the birds sing, Beatrice?

Sing! Sing!

BEATRICE. I don't know. Francis.

Francis, we're leaving.

JOHN JNR *enters* (*inside*).

Francis, go and wait outside.

FRANCIS. I thought we were leaving?

BEATRICE. Francis!

FRANCIS *leaves* (*outside*).

JOHN JNR. Well. Welcome to The White Horse.

BEATRICE. Thank you.

JOHN JNR. I'd offer you a drink but it's not my pub.

BEATRICE. That's not the kind of concern you've ever displayed before.

JOHN JNR. No?

BEATRICE. From my experience you take whatever you want.

JOHN JNR. Don't I just?

BEATRICE. And now I know where you get it from. Charming man.

JOHN JNR. Where've you been?

BEATRICE. Nowhere.

JOHN JNR. C'mere.

BEATRICE. No.

She goes to him.

Silently, COCH BACH *enters (inside) and hides out of sight. Listening.*

JOHN JNR *and* BEATRICE *kiss.*

Stop. My brother…

JOHN JNR. He can't see in here.

BEATRICE. If he sees *anything*, he'll tell my father. That's his nature.

JOHN JNR. Tell him what? Not a lot to tell from where I see it.

BEATRICE. I'm sorry, John.

JOHN JNR. Four weeks now. Every Sunday I've been waiting down there. It's bloody cold and all.

BEATRICE. I know

JOHN JNR. And it's bloody damp in that barn.

BEATRICE. What was I supposed to do?

JOHN JNR. I needed you to keep me warm.

BEATRICE. It's not happening, John. I can't do it anymore.

JOHN JNR. We'll find somewhere warmer. Drier, too, hopefully.

BEATRICE. Oh, well why don't we just use my bedroom?

JOHN JNR. Could we?

BEATRICE. Don't be stupid.

JOHN JNR. We'll work something out.

BEATRICE. I'm not sure I can do this anymore. Sneaking about like a criminal.

JOHN JNR. Ah no, *we're* the criminals, aren't we?

BEATRICE. It has to be honest. This isn't honest. This isn't something good. If, if there was some way we could make this proper. Then.

But until then. I'm sorry.

JOHN JNR. I don't believe this.

BEATRICE. Put yourself in my father's position. Why would he allow you to be with his only daughter? He'd need a good reason. You'd need to convince him that you're less… like this. And more like us. And tonight, in front of my father, you chose the wrong side. But you don't have to.

What would you do for me, John? Who do you love more?

JOHN JNR. I. Well

Ah no.

I can't.

Not that.

BEATRICE. My father would never allow this.
My brother would *kill* you simply if he found out.
But
Your father has terrified them. You should see them

JOHN JNR. I would die for you.

BEATRICE. I'm not asking you to.

JOHN JNR. He is my *father*.

BEATRICE. All he needs to do is leave. They'd be happy with that. They'd be ecstatic.

JOHN JNR. I can't ask him to do that.

BEATRICE. Then don't ask him. Listen, John

> You've *got* something. Something you can use against my father and brother. And you're never going to have anything like it again.

> *Use* it. Please.

JOHN JNR. You can't ask me to choose between you and my father.

BEATRICE. I just have.

JOHN JNR. I've been without him for seven years

BEATRICE. You weren't with him before.

> Your father is a criminal, John. And when he had a twelve-year-old son to care for, he savaged an elderly woman so he could rob her of five pounds

JOHN JNR. He was innocent

BEATRICE. And got himself sent to jail for ten years.
> Coming back here is the worst thing he could have done for you. He's brought chaos upon your head.
> The best thing in the world, John. Is if he leaves.
> And we can use this.
> And we could be together.

JOHN JNR.

BEATRICE. But John.
> If he leaves.
> My family wouldn't know you were responsible.
> You would have no. Leverage.
> If *you* were to give him. *To* us.
> *You.*
> My father would be in your debt.

JOHN JNR. He's my dad.

FRANCIS (*off*). Beatrice! Beatrice, I am perishing!

BEATRICE. John, I have to go.

> No?

BEATRICE *goes to leave.*

JOHN JNR. Yes.

BEATRICE. What?

JOHN JNR. Yes.

I'll give you my father.

BEATRICE. Yes?

JOHN JNR. Yes.

What's it matter, I don't even really know him. He's been in prison most of my life.

BEATRICE. John. This will work. I promise you.
Good night.

BEATRICE *leaves* (*outside*).

JOHN JNR *remains*.

JOHN JNR. Home then.
You bloody idiot.

JOHN JNR *leaves* (*outside*).

COCH BACH *stands*.

Looks around him.

Goes to the bar.

While pouring himself a drink...

COCH BACH. And thereupon he set upon the horses and cut off their lips to the teeth, and their ears to their heads, and their tails to their backs, and wherever he could clutch their eyelids he cut them to the very bone. And he maimed the horses thus till there was no use could be made of the horses.

(*To the birds.*) Here that boys? There's gunna be a war.

COCH BACH *drinks*.

End of Act One.

ACT TWO

The Punishments of Coch Bach y Bala

September thirtieth, six p.m. Tuesday.

The White Horse.

HELEDD *is behind the bar.* JOHN JNR *and* TOMOS *sit.* JOHN JNR *drinks.*

HELEDD *and* JOHN JNR *are lost in their own unhappiness.* TOMOS *is bored of their unhappiness/silence.*

TOM. Right.

Well

JOHN JNR. Shut up, Tomos.

TOM. (*God…*)

I mean

Maybe he's coming back?

I mean, why would he break out of prison, spend two minutes here and then go again? He'll come back. He's lying low.

It's only been a couple of days.

He'll come back, you'll see. And then

HELEDD. Shut up, Tomos.

TOMOS. (*Jesus…*)

We hear him before we see him but… SION *charges in* (*outside*), *dragging a sack. The sack is filled with something big and extremely heavy. It is fighting and kicking.* SION's *hand is bleeding heavily.*

SION. I got it! I got it! Make way!

TOMOS. Ah brilliant! *Something.*

SION. I got him. Make way!

HELEDD. *Sion*!

SION. Careful, careful.

SION *dumps the sack. It twitches and rustles.*

JOHN JNR. What is it?

SION. Well

HELEDD. Ah don't you dare tell me

TOMOS. What IS IT?

SION. S'a

S'badger.

JOHN JNR. Badger?

TOMOS. In there?

SION. Yeah.

JOHN JNR. Looks like a

TOMOS. A

JOHN JNR. A big badger.

SION. It *is* a big badger. That's what it is. A bloody great big badger.

JOHN JNR. Nice.

HELEDD. Oh Sion. Why?

TOMOS. *Brilliant.*

SION. This is the bugger that's been at our cattle.

TOMOS. I thought Mam said

JOHN JNR. What's it been doing?

SION. What's it been doing? Attacking 'em. Biting 'em.

HELEDD. *That* one, is it?

SION. Yes.

HELEDD. That exact badger?

SION. This is no ordinary badger.

JOHN JNR. No?

SION. No.

JOHN JNR. Why not?

SION. It's massive.

TOMOS. It *is* massive, Dad.

HELEDD. Sion, I don't want to sound

SION. This badger. Heledd. Has been *tormenting* our cows. For months. They've been unsettled, scared, unable to give milk. You've seen it. Some gone lame from their bites. This badger is a villain.

It must be punished.

JOHN JNR. Why didn't you just shoot it, Sion?

SION. I want justice done.

HELEDD. Oh what, you want it put in prison with John's father, do you?

JOHN JNR. He's not *in* prison. We don't know where he is.

SION. Don't be stupid, Heledd. You can't put a badger in prison.

I want it hanged.

TOM. Hanged?

SION. I'm not a barbarian, Tomos. When someone wrongs me, I don't chase him through fields with a shotgun. If a man was to murder, he would be hanged.
I am going to hang the badger.
That. Is the only right thing to do.

HELEDD. And then all the other badgers will know.
'Don't bite Sion's cows!'
Maybe they'll have a meeting.

TOM. She's right, Dad. It's not going to help.

SION. This badger is costing our livelihood.

JOHN JNR. It's cruel, Sion.

SION. Cruel? Have you seen what this animal has done?

HELEDD. Animal, Sion. *Animal*.

Anyway, why have you brought this trouble into the pub?
Can't you take Tomos and sort it out?

SION. Tomos?

No. Tomos? Help out on the farm?

Oh, no he's too busy

TOMOS. Dad...

SION. Up in the woods. Having his shooting practice with his
lordship. Too good to muck out the cows now, isn't he? I tell
you, that boy couldn't hit an elephant with a blunderbuss and
he thinks he's going into the army? It's nonsense, nonsense
he's filling that boy's head with.

TOMOS. I could have practised on the badger.

SION. No. It is to be hanged.
Where's that rope?

HELEDD. Sion, look at your hand.

SION. It's nothing. Where's that rope?

JOHN JNR. That's a nasty bite, Sion.

HELEDD. Sion, will you listen?

SION. The badger will be hanged.

JOHN JNR. You want justice, Sion?

SION. Right, I do. Damn right.

JOHN JNR. And this badger's the guilty party?

SION. None other.

JOHN JNR. Before a murderer is hanged, Sion

HELEDD. A *trial*.

JOHN JNR. A trial.

SION. Don't be daft, you can't put a badger on trial.

HELEDD. Why not?

JOHN JNR. You want it hanged, Sion, it should have a trial.

SION. Hang on
You're right. No, that's proper. We'll have a trial.
But it better be found guilty.

HELEDD. Yes. Right, well. Not what I was planning to do with
the evening but there we are.

TOMOS. Busy evening of moping about planned, I suppose.

HELEDD *and* SION *both feel this remark but ignore it.*

SION. How do we do it?

JOHN JNR. Well, we need someone to act as a judge.

SION. The vicar?

TOMOS. Let's go get him!

SION. Alright, alright.

Where is he?

JOHN JNR. The church…?

TOMOS. Yeah. He's always there.

SION. Right, right. Come on then. Let's get that vicar and hang
that bastard badger.

HELEDD. I'll stay here. Guard the bastard badger.

TOMOS. Badger on trial! Yes!

HELEDD. Thanks, John.

TOMOS. Oh, Dad.

SION. What now?

TOMOS. Reginald did ask if we could go and see him. Said he had something for us.

SION. That bloody man

JOHN JNR. I'll get vicar, boys. See you back here.

TOMOS, JOHN JNR and SION leave (outside).

HELEDD looks at the badger.

HELEDD. What next, Heledd Pritchard?

A distant, loud noise. Scraping, rumbling. Getting closer. Something big.

Yep.

She goes to the door and looks out.

Sweet mother of Christ.

Through the door comes COCH BACH (outside). He is dragging an enormous cauldron, taller than a man. It seems impossible that he is able to drag it. He has exerted an enormous amount of strength and is on the brink of collapse. He is even more disheveled, dirty, bloodied and bruised than in Act One. The cauldron barely makes it through the door without smashing the door frame. He drags it into the middle of the pub, knocking chairs and tables aside. It is a thing of wonder. If nothing else, it is enormous.

COCH BACH. It's heavier than it looks.
    I'm back!
    Again.

HELEDD. Hello…

COCH BACH. What?

HELEDD.

COCH BACH. Oh, this? Brightens the place up. Where d'you want it?

HELEDD. What. The hell. Is that, John?

COCH BACH. S'a cauldron.

HELEDD. And where did you get it?

COCH BACH. I stole it

HELEDD. You hardly needed to tell me that. Stole it from *who*?

COCH BACH. The Irish. Well, I borrowed it really.
   Borrowed without asking.

HELEDD. The..?

COCH BACH. Irish. Ireland. I stole it from Ireland.
   S'why I've been away a few days. Had to drag this heavy
   bugger back with me.

HELEDD. You've dragged that. All the way from Ireland? By
   yourself?

COCH BACH. Yes. Ireland.

   We're brothers, the Irish and us. We gave them this cauldron,
   in friendship, a long time ago. They weren't using it. So I've
   brought it back. It's fair enough really.

HELEDD. Well, you'll have to get me more than a pheasant or
   two if we're going to fill that, John love.

COCH BACH. Aye, well, I would have got here a lot quicker,
   except I could only travel at night, on account of the fact that
   I was dragging a six-foot cauldron and people would have
   had questions.

HELEDD. What is it, a peace offering?

COCH BACH. A war drum.

HELEDD. Of course it is.

   COCH BACH *bangs his hands against the cauldron.*

COCH BACH. There's not much left, Heledd. Even this I had
   to drag from the bottom of a lake. The rest is gone. All gone.
   There are bits and bobs, flotsam and jetsam. But not much.
   We'll have to make more history ourselves.

HELEDD. You might not want to make such a racket, there's them that's looking for you.

COCH BACH. Everyone's looking for me.

HELEDD. And don't you just like that, eh.

COCH BACH. Keeps me busy.

HELEDD. Now, what are we going to do with your big pot?

COCH BACH. We're going to win, Heledd. We're going to *win*.

This is just the start of it.

HELEDD. I've no idea what you're talking about but you do liven things up, John. I'll give you that.

COCH BACH. The sea was tricky

HELEDD. I imagine. Wet, was it?

COCH BACH. But I did have some help dragging it onto land, onto the beach at Harlech. A huge fella. Eight foot tall. Clad head to toe in armour.
Took one look at my cauldron
'Where's the fight at?' he said.
'There's no fight for you ' I said. 'Not anymore. Sorry lad.'
'That's right,' he said. 'Ah, that's right.'
And he walked. Straight into the sea.
'You'll get rusty,' I shouted after him.
'Blubbllee blubblee blubrrrlbu blurbrbr,' he replied. No idea what he was saying, his head was underwater.

HELEDD. You don't have to tell me your stories, John.

COCH BACH. Stories? I've never spoken anything but the truth to you. Every word.

HELEDD. I can think of one or two things you said that have yet to happen.

COCH BACH. Aye. Well.

Things, eh?

HELEDD. Things left right and centre, John.

COCH BACH. Aye
   Fourteen you were. Fourteen. And. *Sparkling*.

HELEDD. And you were twenty and should have known better.
   Sparkling, eh?

COCH BACH. I knew. I knew alright.
   And I could think of nothing better.

HELEDD. Don't sparkle so much anymore, do I?

COCH BACH. No.

HELEDD. What charm…

COCH BACH. I'm a thief, Heledd. I steal the sparkling things.
   Just *because* they sparkle. I don't know what I'm going to
   do with them after I've stolen them. I don't need them. I just
   want them.

   You don't sparkle anymore, Heledd. But you sing to me.

HELEDD. I don't know what you're talking about John Jones
   but do shut up and give us a kiss.

COCH BACH. Fair enough.

   They kiss, briefly.

   A knock at the door. They separate. COCH BACH *hides.*

   WINSTANLEY *enters* (*outside*)*. He seems oblivious to the
   six-foot cauldron.*

WINSTANLEY. Good evening, Heledd.

HELEDD. Hello, Constable. Come to inspect all my nooks and
   crannies again, have you?

WINSTANLEY.
   Yes.

HELEDD. Well, we've not seen hide nor hair of Coch Bach.
   Nor pheasant neither.

   Same as yesterday. And the day before.

WINSTANLEY. I'll just have a quick check if that's all the same. Sorry to disturb you, Heledd. Please, carry on. Carry on doing your

Stuff. Chores.

WINSTANLEY *starts to look about.* COCH BACH *has fun at his expense, moving around, constantly one step ahead, sometimes hiding behind* WINSTANLEY, *pinching* HELEDD*'s bottom, generally amusing himself.* WINSTANLEY *never notices him. Or the cauldron.*

It's true enough, there's been no sign of Coch Bach. Even young Reginald is starting to believe he's gone.

HELEDD. Oh he's gone, alright.

WINSTANLEY. It's a good job. A very good job.

HELEDD. Oh yeah?

WINSTANLEY. The Jones-Batemans, Heledd. They were taking all of this very seriously. Talking about pressing to have Coch hanged if they found him.

HELEDD. Oh, don't you start on about hanging as well.

WINSTANLEY. What? Oh, they were deadly serious.

HELEDD. You're the police, Eifion. It's your decision. You'd have him hanged would you?

WINSTANLEY. I don't decide. I don't decide what are crimes and what aren't. And I don't decide what punishments are given. I just do my job.

Do you know when I last saw Coch Bach? There was a riot in Bala, years ago, few weeks before he was arrested. Police from all over were called in so I was there with a few others, and there was this mob, ugly thing it was, tearing things up, setting fires. Hurling anything they could get their hands on. All the shop fronts had their windows smashed, a pregnant woman got hit with half a brick I remember. At one point we were face to face with these thugs, going hand to hand, and I was wrestling with this one muscly little rogue. Suddenly, I realise that the man I was grappling with was Coch.

My friend.

So I let him go. 'Coch!' I say. 'Coch, what are you doing?'
And he looks me dead in the eye. 'Piss off, Copper.'
He says.
And he spits in my face.
Knows exactly who I am.
Rather he'd struck me and knocked me out cold.

HELEDD. Well, we all have our memories of him.

WINSTANLEY. Well! Not here, is he? Mind if I check upstairs, Heledd?

COCH BACH *comes out from his hiding place.*

COCH BACH. HOW HAVE YOU NOT NOTICED THE CAULDRON?

IT'S TEN FOOT TALL.

WINSTANLEY. Coch! You *are* here.

WINSTANLEY *looks at the cauldron. Turns to* HELEDD.

You've got an enormous cauldron there, Heledd.

COCH BACH *strikes* WINSTANLEY *over the head with a bottle knocking him unconscious.*

HELEDD. John!

COCH BACH. He said that's what he'd rather. Didn't spit on him, did I?

HELEDD. You've assaulted a *police*man.

COCH BACH. I've assaulted a lot of policemen. Beyond prison breaks and stealing enormous, slightly unbelievable objects, it's sort of my trademark.

Anything important in the sack?

HELEDD. A badger.

COCH BACH. A…?

HELEDD. A badger.

COCH BACH. Well that's new.

HELEDD. It's a long story.

> COCH BACH *unties the bag*

> Careful, it's alive and vicious.

> COCH BACH *drags the badger out. It's dead.*

COCH BACH. Not anymore it isn't.
You alive, pal?
Nope.

HELEDD. Sion brought it in. Bit his hand something terrible.

COCH BACH. Aye, well I'd bite the hand of the horror who
was trying to put me in a sack.

HELEDD. Reckons it was the one terrorising the cattle.

COCH BACH. Oh yeah? Like the mice that were terrorising the
crops? Or the ladybirds that were eating the manure?

HELEDD. It *is* very big…

COCH BACH. Tomos is better off in the army, if you ask
me. There's nothing in these hills for a lad. Sheep shit and
shagging. That's all.

HELEDD. Yes, well, Sion *would* ask you.
And sheep shit and shagging seemed to do you alright.

COCH BACH. Yeah, well I'm a man of simple pleasures.

> COCH BACH *picks up the badger and, as carefully as he
> can, drops it in the cauldron.*

> (*To the badger.*) Sorry, fella.

> (*To* HELEDD.) Give us a hand.

> *Together they put* WINSTANLEY *into the sack and re-tie.
> They put the sack back where it was.*

HELEDD. Aiding an escaped convict, well I never...

COCH BACH. Helping a friend.

HELEDD. Eifion is my friend.

COCH BACH. That's what I meant.
Now.
Where were we?

They kiss.

Noises outside.

HELEDD. Shh!
Come on.

They scamper off, upstairs (inside).

REGINALD, TOMOS *and* SION *enter (outside).*
REGINALD *carries a gleaming hunting rifle.*

REGINALD. No. No! Sion, a soldier must have a weapon. It
is my pleasure to gift this to Tom. It's a matter of honour,
Tom. I look after my troops. Ask the men in my regiment. I
look after them. And I always buy them a beer. You can ask
them. I –

They look at the cauldron.

I say.

SION. Heledd!

Heledd, what is this doing in our inn?

Heledd!

She must be out.

TOMOS. What is it?

SION. I have no idea.

REGINALD. Wives!
Well, landlord, whatever it is, my soldier and I demand ale.

SION. Yep, yep. Coming up.

REGINALD. And one for yourself of course.
Always show generosity, Tom. That's a lesson.

SION *goes behind the bar to pour the beer. They make themselves comfortable.*

I'm going to ask for you to be put into my regiment, Tom.
Third Battalion, Royal Welsh.

TOMOS. Great.

REGINALD. I insisted, you know? They wanted to put me in a regiment that – how did they phrase it? – that would 'more suit a man of my background'. But no, I said. I live here and I want to fight shoulder to shoulder with men from the Vale of Clwyd. It. Makes me proud. It does, it really does.

TOMOS. Where have you fought?

REGINALD. Well, nowhere yet. Not really. But we've *trained* together. We've suffered together.

'If you can keep your head when all about you are losing theirs.'

You know?

SION. And you're a captain? In the regiment?

REGINALD. '*If you can force your heart and nerve and sinew*'
Of course.
Yes. I know. You can imagine what they think of me.

TOMOS. What?

REGINALD. Um…

SION. That you're a posh English so-and-so?

REGINALD. I hardly think they're that polite. They're not even that polite to my face, goodness knows what they say behind my back.

SION. I wouldn't worry. You could be their own brother and soon as you's in charge, they'd turn on you. Men round here don't like being told what to do. That's all.

TOMOS. Don't they *like* you?

REGINALD. We're getting there. First I have to earn their respect before they like me.

TOMOS. Oh. They respect you.

REGINALD. No. But we're getting there. I've spent time with them

But

We just a need a *war*. It would really help

Nothing binds men together like a war. And the Serbs are spoiling for one. I don't trust the Huns either.

SION. How's that then, Tomos? Fancy going to war?

TOMOS. Yeah.

SION. Well you'd better toughen up a bit then. Pick up a shovel, work the land. Put some meat on you.

REGINALD *notices the tension.*

REGINALD. Quite right. Quite right, you should keep working hard on the farm, Tom. Make a man of you. All those. Bales of hay. And. Ploughs.

TOMOS (*angry at his father*). I will.

REGINALD. Enjoy your beer?

TOMOS. Yes, thank you.

REGINALD. Another?

TOMOS. No. Thank you. John, John Jnr needs my help with something.

REGINALD. Good man. What a good man. Eh, Sion?

SION. Aye.

REGINALD. Don't forget this.

REGINALD *hands* TOMOS *the rifle.*

TOMOS. Thank you, Mr Jones-Bateman.

REGINALD. Reginald. Please.

TOMOS. Reginald.

Bye.

REGINALD. Thank you, Tom.

TOMOS *leaves (outside).* SION *plucks up his courage.*

SION. You know, Mr Jones-Bateman. I've only got one son.

I'd like him to be here.

REGINALD. The farm.

Sion, if I can be impolite. It's a small holding. You have a few cows.

Now, the army will make a man of Tom. And when he's done, maybe there will be a farm waiting for him. That's your responsibility. He'll return a man. And make it *his* farm. Build him something he can be proud of.

We own this land, Sion. And I can't promise a young man he can make his living off this land.

But I can in the army.

SION. Well. He's certainly keen.

REGINALD. Hhm.

I can't find John Jones, Sion.

SION. No?

REGINALD. I can't find John Jones

And I feel humiliated.

SION. Well he's

REGINALD. He's not gone.

SION. No?

REGINALD. Yes, there's no sign of him on the land. Or here. But he's somewhere.

SION. You think he's still around?

REGINALD. Oh yes. He's a clever man, you know that. He's a step ahead of us. I don't know his secret. But someone does.

SION. Oh yeah?

REGINALD. I *trust* you, Sion.

SION. Yeah? Good. Thanks. That's, yeah.

REGINALD. Do you trust me?

SION. Sure. Yeah.

REGINALD. Why do you love John Jones so much? I don't mean just you – everyone.

SION. Oh. Well

REGINALD. I can't see it. What's he ever done for any of you? He's not particularly amusing…

SION. He's. A friend. Yunno?

REGINALD. Right, right. I'm going to cut to the chase, Sion.

John Jones was having his way with your wife before he was imprisoned. Everyone knows that. I mean before he was imprisoned last time round. From what I gather they were childhood sweethearts and her marriage to you didn't seem to unduly bother them.

What a thing.

So.

He's back. Where does that leave you? Landlord?

He's back for good.

Someone's going to have to, oh what? Deliver him to me? Not physically. But deliver him. To me.

Some*one* will have to

Look, he's under our noses but we can't catch a whiff of his scent. He simply cannot be doing this by himself, he must be having some help. And, I think, rather a lot of help. That little scene the other night was enough to tell me where all your loyalties lie. So.

Eventually, Sion, he's going to need your help. Or Heledd's. More likely Heledd's, eh? But she's still your wife and I assume you share. Something.

The point being, at some point, Sion, you're going to know his whereabouts.

Hopefully it won't be between your wife's legs.

And when you do know his whereabouts.

So will I.

SION.

REGINALD. Have a think?

SION. Yeah.

REGINALD. Good man.

You *are* a good man.

He's not.

Let's celebrate that.

Good evening, Sion.

SION. Evening.

REGINALD *leaves* (*outside*).

SION *looks at the cauldron.*

Bastard.

SION *tries to drag the cauldron outside. It won't budge.*

HELEDD *enters* (*inside*), *mildly startled to see* SION.

HELEDD. Oh

What are you trying to do, Sion?

SION. Nothing.

SION *leaves (outside), bumping into… BEATRICE, who enters (outside)*.

HELEDD. Oh hello, love.

BEATRICE. Is it inconvenient? I can come back.

HELEDD. No, no. It's fine. Thank you for coming.

BEATRICE (*looking at the cauldron*). It's remarkable.

HELEDD. Oh, this old thing? Aye she's a fine
Pot.

BEATRICE. This might sound impertinent. But you cook for a lot of people, don't you? I mean, you feed. You feed lots of people.

HELEDD. I do my bit. Do my best. It's not anything

BEATRICE. My father says you're poor. But. You aren't poor. Not really.

HELEDD. Oh. No. No, of course not. We get by just fine.

BEATRICE. I mean. You are.

Sorry this is embarrassing.

I grew up in India. And. People are poor there. I mean, poor.

HELEDD. I'm sure.

BEATRICE. Oh God, I sound frightful. What I mean to say is. What do I mean to say?
I just find it hard. That some people here go hungry. Do they? In the village?

HELEDD. Maybe we could talk about Tomos?

BEATRICE. Of course. Yes.

Maybe we could just

No, no. Sorry.

HELEDD. No, go on.

BEATRICE. I just wondered. Sorry. Just one moment.

Sorry.

BEATRICE *pulls a chair up to the cauldron and stands upon the chair. She looks inside the cauldron.*

Oh!

HELEDD. What is it?

BEATRICE. Oh gosh, I am so sorry.

HELEDD. What?

BEATRICE. Oh no. I didn't realise it was that. Bad.

HELEDD. What is, now?

BEATRICE. The badger.

HELEDD. Ah.

BEATRICE. How can we be so cruel? I knew that you sometimes fed some families in the village. It doesn't escape our attention that some children here would occasionally go hungry if it wasn't for you

HELEDD. Everyone pitches in, love. If fifty people need feeding, it only takes a handful to make supper. You'd be amazed what can be made to stretch.

BEATRICE. But, Heledd. A badger!

HELEDD. What, well we're not going to eat th–

BEATRICE. Women in India would scavenge for anything they could. Even animals killed on the rails. But I didn't know… Not here!

Heledd, I cannot let you eat badger. I cannot let the children of this village eat badger! It is beastly

HELEDD. Beatrice, I don't think

BEATRICE. You poor people! It is a sin to eat a badger.

HELEDD (*sensing her opportunity*). Is it? Yes! Yes it is. And we are *ashamed*! Oh Beatrice, it is terrible. Many nights we have fed the whole village on a single badger. Or a hedgehog. Or a squirrel. This is what it is like. You don't understand.

BEATRICE. It breaks my heart. We live in such luxury

HELEDD. Do you see? Do you understand why Tomos must go into the army?

BEATRICE. I do, I do!

HELEDD. My son deserves better than this.

BEATRICE. Heledd, I shall do everything I can. I will.
I will speak to my father and make sure he understands how important it is for Tomos to join the regiment.

HELEDD. Thank you, Beatrice. Thank you.

BEATRICE. But I cannot stand here and let children eat a foul badger for their supper this evening. I had no idea. Really I didn't. No idea. I will do something.

My brother said he would be coming by, do you mind if I wait in the warm for him?

HELEDD. Of course. You're a kind soul, Beatrice.

BEATRICE. I try.

HELEDD. I have to get on. Lots of people to feed. Good evening.

BEATRICE. Good evening, Heledd!

HELEDD *leaves* (*outside*)*, leaving* BEATRICE.

She can't resist, so stands on the chair to look inside the cauldron again. She looks just over the edge. She screams and moves away.

Out of the cauldron climbs COCH BACH.

BEATRICE *tries to get out of the door.* COCH BACH *catches her. She screams.* COCH BACH *clamps his hand over her mouth and pacifies her. Gently.*

COCH BACH. Shush. Shush, now. Hush, now, love. Please. Come on now. I'm not going to hurt you.

BEATRICE *quietens, if not calms, down.*

Hush, hush, hush.

Eh? What was good?

Your little brother thinks I'm no Houdini, but that was pretty good, right?

Don't panic, I'm not going to hurt you.

I'm going to let you go. You with me?

He does.

Better?

BEATRICE. You've been here three days. You might have had a bath.

COCH BACH. I had splash in the Irish Sea just yesterday.

BEATRICE. We thought you had gone

John thought

One word to my brother…

COCH BACH. Very true.

BEATRICE. What do you want?

COCH BACH. A crown. And a throne. A big horse.

But right now?

I want my son to be happy. What a sap I am, eh?

BEATRICE. Is he not happy?

COCH BACH. He's as miserable as sin. And it's your fault.

BEATRICE. Mine? I don't see why that would

COCH BACH. I heard your little chat the other night.

BEATRICE. Oh

COCH BACH. Asking a man to sell his own father down the river? Tut tut tut.

BEATRICE. Give me one good reason why I shouldn't scream the place down.

COCH BACH. Go on then.

BEATRICE. Reginald will be here at any moment.

COCH BACH. HEEEEEEEELPPPPPPPPP

Yeah? Like that?

SOMEOOOONE OH GOD

I'VE BEEN APPREHENDED BY A NOTORIOUS AND
SOMEWHAT PUNGENT ESCAPED CONVICT

Who knows what he could want?

Maybe we could pray together?

BEATRICE. Very amusing.

COCH BACH. I just wanted to talk. If you're planning to make
an honourable man of my only son I think you'd give me
that right.

BEATRICE. Oh, pah. You want to know what my intentions are
for your son?

COCH BACH. Aye.

BEATRICE. Want to know what the dowry might be?

COCH BACH. What do I look like, love? Your father would
sooner give me you than a penny of his own money.
No. I want what you want.
Don't I?

BEATRICE. How am I supposed to know what a man like you
could possibly want?

COCH BACH. Because I told you two minutes ago.

BEATRICE. Well John *will* be happy once you flutter off again.

COCH BACH. I don't know. I've been away the last few days
and I see that he's about as happy as a pig without a
He's unhappy.
And you'd love that to be my fault, but it's yours.
Stringing him along

BEATRICE. That isn't fair

COCH BACH. Stringing him along. YES IT IS FAIR.
Yes it is.
You promised him the earth and now you spit on him.

BEATRICE. And what do you suggest? That we elope?

COCH BACH. No. No, you'll marry. At Cynfarch's place.
And I'll give you the finest wedding present anyone could
bestow upon anyone.
Me.

BEATRICE. You'll. What?

COCH BACH. You're a cunning thing. I like you. I heard every
word of your plan and I loved it.
John captures the ogre. Turns him over. The hero marries
the blushing beauty. Like the legends. The grateful king,
promising his most beautiful daughter to the first man who
can slay the dragon. Very nice.

BEATRICE. And why would you do that?

COCH BACH. Why? I want my boy to have his birthright. I
want him to have this land.

BEATRICE. Surely. Your Highness. You could simply bequeath
it to him. Is he not heir to your invisible throne?

COCH BACH. There's nothing wrong with a story, love.
I may be a fool but I'm not a bloody fool. My blood deserves
some stake in this land.

BEATRICE. The land will go to Reginald. And my father isn't a
king. He's owns a few fields.

COCH BACH. My fields.
Some stake. Is all I want. Is all I can hope for.

BEATRICE. Even if John hands you over, there's no assurance
my father would suddenly believe he is an appropriate
match.

COCH BACH. He will once I've finished. Your father hasn't a
clue what I am capable of. But he will. And by then he would
sell you a thousand times over to a Turkish whorehouse if it
meant seeing the back of me.

My son can't be a landowner. But his sons can.
Help me.

BEATRICE. Very well. If you want to do it like that, let's get
John now and sort this out.

COCH BACH. Now isn't the time. As I said, your father still
needs convincing that I'm a man he *really* wants shot of.
John can't be a hero if I'm just an ogre. I need to be a
monster.
No, keep it quiet for now. Even from John. John can't know.
He has to, he has to believe it too.
Give me a few hours maybe.

BEATRICE. If this is a trick

COCH BACH. Aye, I do lots of tricks. But you hold all the
cards, eh?
One false move? You're the man swinging the axe, Beatrice
love. I'm just the chopping block. Hold firm.

BEATRICE. Because it could work.

COCH BACH. Oh I know.

BEATRICE. Well. I feel perfectly guilty already.

COCH BACH. There is one more thing. Partner.

BEATRICE. What?

COCH BACH. It's a small, small favour considering what
you're getting in return. My son for a small, small, small
thing. A tiny thing.

BEATRICE. Yes?

COCH BACH. I need something.

COCH BACH *hands* BEATRICE *a scrap of paper.*

That.

BEATRICE. It's a
Map? No
A drawing.
Of?
Oh. Oh no…

COCH BACH. Yes.

BEATRICE. I *can't*.

COCH BACH. Well.

BEATRICE. I can't. I just can't. It's impossible.

COCH BACH. Try.

BEATRICE. I can try.

COCH BACH. He mustn't know. Keep it secret.
Eh, and you're family now. No such thing as can't in this
clan.
Especially when it comes to thieving.
You're alright you are.

COCH BACH *leaves* (*inside*).

BEATRICE *watches him leave. Waits. Thinks. Carefully
approaches the cauldron, stands on the chair, and very, very
slowly peeks over the edge. But before she can, in comes*
TOMOS, JOHN JNR, SION *and* GERAINT (*outside*). *She
jumps down.*

SION....if anything I think I'm being *too* reasonable
Oh. Hello, Miss Jones-Bateman.

BEATRICE. Hello. Hello, John.

TOMOS. Is that your, er, cauldron?

BEATRICE. Oh. No. No, no, it's Heledd's. Of course. You
know that.
Her special big pot. For the village. You know.

TOMOS. Right. Yeah. Brill. Big pot.

JOHN JNR. Can we help you? Miss Jones-Bateman.

BEATRICE. Um. No, I was talking with Heledd actually, Sion.

SION. Oh yeah, what about?

BEATRICE. Village gossip.

TOMOS. Women do love to gossip. This much I know.

GERAINT. You know so very little.

JOHN JNR. Well. Best be off then.

BEATRICE. Yes. I was just waiting

JOHN JNR. We're very busy.

BEATRICE. Sounds interesting. What are you up to?

JOHN JNR. Village business.

BEATRICE. Well I live in

JOHN JNR. Village. Business.

BEATRICE. Yes.
My mother will need help anyway. Good evening,
gentlemen.

SION. Evening, Miss.

GERAINT. Good evening, girl.

BEATRICE *leaves* (*outside*).

Where's this bloody badger then?

SION. In the sack. Bugger nearly took my hand off getting him
in there.

GERAINT. Let us begin.

JOHN JNR. *Bring forth the accused!*

GERAINT. John. This is no laughing matter. The badger must
have a fair trial.

JOHN JNR. And to think, only last week my cousin asked me if
I didn't get bored living round here.

TOMOS. Dad, what's with the, whatever it is? Big saucepan.

SION. Dunno. It's your mam's, isn't it.
You know, wives.

GERAINT. Order, order.
Court is in session.
Will the complainant please make himself known?

SION. That is me.

GERAINT. Your name?

SION. Sion Pritchard.

GERAINT. And your complaint?

SION. I wish for this badger to be hung by the neck until dead

JOHN JNR. That's the punishment not the complaint.

SION. I was getting to that. The complaint? Months of terrorism in my fields. Biting cattle, scaring cattle, assaulting sheep.

And look at my hand!

TOMOS. You really should get that seen to, Dad.

GERAINT. And is this badger present?

SION. Yes, your honour, in the sack there.

GERAINT. Name?

SION. Sion Pritchard, your honour.

GERAINT. What is the name of the *accused*?

SION. I didn't think to name it.

TOMOS. Mr Badger.

SION. It's anonymous.

GERAINT. Then Mr Badger will suffice.

TOMOS. *Yes!*

SION. Mr Badger?

GERAINT. Hush! As the accused, Mr Badger, is a badger. Who will speak for him?

TOMOS. I will!

GERAINT. Not you.

JOHN JNR. I'll do it.

GERAINT. You understand, John, that means you must defend Mr Badger's actions?

JOHN JNR. I understand.

SION. Give him hell, John. Send him down.

JOHN JNR. That's, that's not how defence works, Sion. I think that bite's starting to make you confused.

GERAINT. Silence! Mr Pritchard, what are your reasons for demanding such a harsh punishment for the accused?

TOMOS (*quietly*). He's mental?

GERAINT. Hssht!

SION. Well, your honour

JOHN JNR. (Your honour…)

SION. I have lost three good cows to bites from the badger and half my herd have stopped producing milk because of the threat of violence hanging over their heads. He is a constant menace to my livestock. And look at my hand!

GERAINT. Your hand is indeed manky.
Mr Jones, what have you to say to save the accused from the hangman? His crimes are notorious indeed.

JOHN JNR. Ahem.
Well, your honour, ladies and gentlemen of the – pub. I am shocked to hear us discuss the accused, Mr Badger, as if his guilt were already in no doubt

SION. It *is* in no doubt!

GERAINT. Shush.

JOHN JNR. It isn't.

GERAINT. Shush! But also carry on.

JOHN JNR. Mr Pritchard claims that Mr Badger is indeed the very same badger that has been causing a merry mischief amongst his cattle. But how do we know?

SION. It bloody is! It's massive!

GERAINT. Order!

JOHN JNR. Your honour, as the accused has no voice, I ask permission to assume his voice. So that the jury may better understand my argument.

GERAINT. You may.

TOMOS. This just gets better and better.

JOHN JNR. I am a humble badger

SION. He's taking the piss.

JOHN JNR. I'm not.

GERAINT. Continue.

JOHN JNR. A humble badger

SION. That's not what badgers sound like.

TOMOS. Yeah, they have deeper voices.

GERAINT. Order in court!
    Continue.

JOHN JNR. I have a wife

TOMOS. (Mrs Badger)

JOHN JNR. And cubs to care for. It has been unseasonably cold over the last few weeks. Times are hard for us badgers. Is it unreasonable, when my cubs are starving, to look for food? And when food cannot be found, to look further afield?

If the ground is too hard to dig for worms and grubs, and the smaller animals are burrowed away, hiding from the cold. Us badgers will, I admit, look longingly through fences and hedgerows. Our empty bellies rumbling. Our cubs weak from hunger. Our limbs aching from a lack of sustenance. And there, for others but not for us, food. Sheep, cattle, meat. Mere metres away.

But what *evidence* do you have? Devoured carcasses?

Skeletons picked clean? Animals disappeared altogether? No. Small bites. Scratches. A spooked mare or two. Have I done this? Consider. First I have to negotiate the fence. If I somehow bite my way through, and I somehow scrape my way through the barbed wire without taking off half my hide. Then, I risk the farmer's shotgun. And the farmer's son's hunting rifle. And the farmer's wife's pitchfork. And once amongst the cattle, the hard hooves of dozens of animals twice our size, the horns, the hot breath. Surrounded.

I risk all this? I survive all this? For a quick bite? A little scratch, your honour? Would I do something like that, like that, for a quick bite? I am a ferocious creature. I could drag home two cows at a time, your honour. What would I need with a quick bite of a leg?

GERAINT. He's got a point, by God.

TOMOS. Poor Mr Badger.

SION. It's not *real*! That was John, not the badger.

TOMOS. And his poor little cubs. Starving away like that, Dad.

SION. That's not how a badger thinks! And this is your farm, Tomos

JOHN JNR. How does a badger think then, Sion?

SION. I'm not sure they do John and that's half their problem.

JOHN JNR. I don't know how you have the heart to hang a badger after that moving testimony, Vicar.

SION. Testimony?! Look at my hand! That's testimony.

GERAINT. I have already come to my decision.

SION. Shouldn't we have a vote?

JOHN JNR. Well, let's hear the Vicar's thoughts first. Then we can decide if we agree.

TOMOS. I'm not letting you hang Mr Badger, Dad. What would Mrs Badger do?

GERAINT. Sion, I understand your desire for vengeance

SION. Do you? Badger bitten and scared off half your parishioners, has it?

GERAINT. I sympathise, Sion

SION. You think *my* wife isn't suffering? You think *my* child doesn't go hungry?
And I've done *nothing* wrong.

GERAINT. Hanging the badger is too severe, Sion. And you know that.

But. There must be some punishment. I take Sion's word when he says that this is the badger who has been causing mischief on his land. So. There must be something done. And everyone here has an opinion. And everyone should have a say.

When I were a boy, we would often play 'beat the badger'.

JOHN JNR. Oh yeah?

TOMOS. Are vicars allowed to do that?

GERAINT. Quiet! Badgers would often cause us trouble. Sometimes their numbers needed thinning. So. We would play beat the badger. A badger would be placed inside a sack, as so. Using a sturdy staff, each person present would deliver a blow to the sack, each striking the badger as hard as they believed was appropriate. But it was crucial that no one blow by an individual should contain sufficient force to cause fatal damage to the animal.

TOMOS. Eh?

GERAINT. You can't kill it.

JOHN JNR. But it might die if it gets enough heavy blows.

GERAINT. That is possible.

JOHN JNR. Tell you what, Vicar, hanging the badger doesn't sound so mad after all.

TOMOS. Yeah, I know you're holy, but that is weird.

GERAINT. It's fair. If the majority feel the punishment should
be lenient, then it will be. Sion?

SION. Fair's fair.

GERAINT. You understand that you must exercise restraint,
Sion? You must not kill the animal.

SION. If that's what everyone thinks is fair.

TOMOS. I think this is the best day I have ever had.

GERAINT. Sion? Have you a staff?

SION. Got a broom.

GERAINT. This will do.

>SION *grabs a broom from behind the bar.* JOHN JNR *drags
>the sack somewhere central.*

Who will be first?

JOHN JNR. Sion?

SION. No. I'll go last.

JOHN JNR. Fair enough.
Here we are.

>JOHN JNR *steps forward with the broom and delivers quite
>a hard blow to the sack which contains* WINSTANLEY.
>WINSTANLEY *makes a grunt that could be easily mistaken
>for an animal.*

TOMOS. Poor thing.

>JOHN JNR *holds the broom out for* TOMOS.

SION. Remember what it's done now, Tomos.

TOMOS. Ah, no…

GERAINT. Everyone present must deliver a blow.

>TOMOS *takes the broom and hits the sack without much
>power. The sack wriggles.*

SION. Oh come on, son.

GERAINT. No, Sion, that is Tomos's judgment.

SION. Well I know where he can go next time he wants a beer.

SION takes the broom and moves to the sack.

GERAINT. The lord is merciful, Sion. Just remember that.

SION. Right, well, he'll probably forgive me this then.

SION strikes the bag with all his might. The sack grunts and stops wriggling.

TOMOS. Hey!

GERAINT. Sion, that was too much. No single blow should

SION. Whoops.

TOMOS. He can't get away with that!

SION. It's still breathing, youth.
And what now, Geraint, we just turn it loose and wait for it to attack my cattle again?

GERAINT. What's done is done.

JOHN JNR. Vicar. You haven't smacked it yet.

GERAINT. Oh no.

SION. Yes, you said everyone must have their go. Come on.

GERAINT. God does not get involved with the affairs of badgers.

REGINALD enters (outside), with a brace of rabbits. SION is still standing over the sack, brandishing the broom.

REGINALD. Good evening, gentlemen.
What's happening here then?

SION. Nothing.

JOHN JNR. Nothing much.

GERAINT. Just a matter that needed sorting.

REGINALD. Right. What's in the sack?

SION. A badger. Mr Jones-Bateman.

REGINALD. Crikey. It's enormous.

SION. It is. Huge. I don't know if you know but there's this
    badger that's been terrorising my cattle

REGINALD. No, no, I heard. Sion, yes. It's, it's no good. And
    you've caught the scoundrel?

SION. Yes. This is he.

TOMOS. Mr Badger.

REGINALD. Pardon?

    HELEDD *enters* (*outside*).

HELEDD. Hello gentlemen
    Oh…

SION. Sorry about the mess, love. We're dealing with the
    badger.

HELEDD. The badger
    In the sack?

SION. Yes.

JOHN JNR. Sion wanted it hanged. Like a criminal. But we're
    beating it in a sack, one by one instead, which is fairer.

REGINALD. Why don't you just kill it?

GERAINT. Justice needs to be done. Each man present delivers
    the blow that he thinks is deserved. If the animal dies, it is
    because we have all deemed it so, not one man.

REGINALD. Marvelous!

HELEDD. You've all been beating the, badger, in the sack?

TOMOS. Aye and Dad gave it such a thump I'm amazed it
    didn't break in two.

HELEDD. Oh heck…

SION. It's a, er, a funny thing Mr Jones-Bateman – but – er –
it's something we decided upon. Seemed fair.

REGINALD. No, no, of course. No, I think it's
If this is what you do then
If this is, the justice that you
Then
Please, carry on.

JOHN JNR. We've finished.

GERAINT. Judgment has been passed.

SION. And the bastard thing is still breathing.

HELEDD. Still breathing! That's wonderful, isn't it?

REGINALD. Well, not everyone present has had their strike.
Have they?
Pass me the stick, Sion. If every man present is allowed to
pass his own judgment, then surely I must too.

HELEDD. Oh no, Mr Jones-Bateman. That's not, not necessary.

REGINALD. No, I must get my hands calloused as much as the
next man in this village.

REGINALD *takes the broom and moves to the sack.*

And I think you'll find, Sion, my sentence is hard. But fair.
You see I can't allow vermin to terrorise the cattle on my
land. One must protect their land from invaders. No matter
how much it might seem that that invader belongs here, is
part of the land, if they are causing harm then you have every
right to rid yourself of them. No matter how hard that might
seem.

HELEDD. Mr Jones-Bateman. I really do think the badger has
suffered enough.

SION. How do you know?

HELEDD. Well, three strong men have struck it. That's enough
surely.

JOHN JNR. Tom basically tickled it.

HELEDD. I cannot stand by and watch you do this.

SION. Go upstairs then.

HELEDD. Mr Jones-Bateman, it's just a dumb animal, it means no harm

TOMOS. I agree!

SION. Heledd, since when have you cared about a bloody badger? You hate them.

HELEDD. I just think that, that God, in front of our vicar here, that God would want us to turn the other cheek. Am I right, Vicar?

GERAINT. God does not involve himself in the aff–

HELEDD. Please don't hit it.

REGINALD. Each man must have his say.

SION. Why shouldn't he?

HELEDD. You might regret it.

REGINALD. Hardly.

REGINALD *deals the sack an almighty blow.*

HELEDD. Oh Jesus!

TOMOS. It's had enough now. Come on. No more. Vicar?

GERAINT. Each man has had his say. Enou–

REGINALD *thumps the sack again, even harder. And again.*

REGINALD. What?
As landowner I thought I should get two votes.

JOHN JNR. That was three.

REGINALD. One was for my father.

HELEDD. Enough, enough! Sion you've had your revenge. Boys, you've all had your fun. Before you make any more mess...

HELEDD *drags the sack behind the bar.*

SION. Thank you, Vicar.
Been hunting, Mr Jones-Bateman?

SION *points at the two rabbits that* REGINALD *brought in.*

REGINALD. Yes. Actually, yes I have. And
These

He hands the rabbits to HELEDD.

are for you.

HELEDD. Thank you…

REGINALD. Courtesy of my young sister.

JOHN JNR. Beatrice?

REGINALD. Well, *I* hunted them. Because Beatrice *insisted.*
And insisted I brought them to you Heledd. For your big pot
there.

SION. That's. Very kind.

REGINALD. Well, we can't have you eating badger, can we?

SION. We weren't planning to.

REGINALD. Don't play coy. It's fine. We understand. Beatrice
saw the badger in the pot. Well, we'll not have you eat
badger any more. This is our land and

SION. The badger's in the bag, sir.

REGINALD. Well, it must be another badger. There's plenty
around. Though, I must say, that badger's big enough to feed
the whole village so I quite understand if it's him for the
stew. He'd be tenderised enough by now anyway, hah!

TOMOS. I'm not eating badger, no way.

REGINALD. In the pot. Beatrice saw it

SION *drags up a chair by the cauldron, stands on it, and
looks inside.*

SION. Jesus

JOHN JNR. What?

SION. There's a massive badger in here.

REGINALD. See! We know, don't be ashamed

JOHN JNR. What badger?

SION. My badger.

TOMOS. What?

>TOMOS *jumps on the chair and looks.*

>It is! Hey hey! Mr Badger's well!
>Well
>Hang on.
>He's not well.

JOHN JNR. Sion. Your badger, the one that's been at your cattle, the one you brought in, is in the pot there?

SION. Yes.

TOMOS. And he's dead.

JOHN JNR. Then what was in the sack?

>*A moment.*

>SION *goes behind the bar and drags the sack back out.*

SION. I left, that badger, in that sack. I *swear*.

JOHN JNR. We saw it, Sion.

TOMOS. Did we?

JOHN JNR. I think so.

GERAINT. Open the sack. And may God forgive you.

SION. Says the man whose idea it was to beat the living daylights of whatever was inside.

REGINALD. What, what is it? Another badger… or, what? What, what's in there?

>JOHN JNR *unties the sack and pulls out a bruised and bloodied, but alive,* WINSTANLEY.

SION. Jesus Christ above, Vicar, and I don't apologise for my language.

TOMOS. I barely hit him! You all saw….

REGINALD. How has this happened? You were beating the constable? And you've tricked me into assaulting him with you. My God…

JOHN JNR. No. No, no, I swear we thought it was the badger. Vicar?

GERAINT. We were *told* it was the badger. John, Tomos, Heledd. We were all told.

SION. Oh come on! Thanks a lot, Geraint, you
Old git.

REGINALD. Sion, what sort of trick is this? Is this because of Tomos?

SION. No, Mr Jones-Bateman, I swear. Eifion is my friend.

REGINALD. Last time I was in this place it didn't look like Constable Winstanley had any friends round here at all.

SION. I wanted that badger dead

REGINALD. It is dead

SION. I wanted it hanged! Not just dead but hanged. I needed to see it die in front of my eyes. I needed everyone to see it. I needed Tomos to see it. I swear to you, I believed that that badger was in the sack. I have no grievance against Eifion. And plenty against the badger.

REGINALD. Then who on earth has done this?
Ah.
Well
I can think of one man who would pull a stunt like this.
Am I right?
Protecting him again.
After this?

SION. We've seen as much of him as you have since the other night. He slept here but was gone before daybreak. We never saw him and we still haven't.

JOHN JNR. He's long gone.

HELEDD. Do you think we could continue this after we've got Eifion to a hospital?

REGINALD. Yes, quite right. I'll take him. John, Tom, could you carry him? I'll get my horses ready.
I will return later.
(*Reminding him.*) Sion?

SION. Yeah, yeah.

REGINALD *leaves* (*outside*). TOMOS *and* JOHN JNR *pick up* WINSTANLEY *and carry him out* (*outside*).

HELEDD. A drink, Vicar? After all that *excitement*?

GERAINT. Not right now. I'm making myself scarce.
God may not interfere with the affairs of man or beast, but he certainly does not go anywhere near the affairs of John bloody Jones.

GERAINT *leaves (outside), leaving* SION *and* HELEDD.

SION. It's funny, isn't it?

HELEDD. What is?

SION. I love John when he's not here. He's everything prigs like Reginald aren't. And he sticks up for me. He sticks up for everyone who needs it.
But when he's here
It's chaos.
I'm getting too old for it, love.
And I know, I know you like it. But did you see Eifion's face?

HELEDD. Yes.

SION. And why? Why? Cos he's a copper? We grew up together, John, Eif and me. He's a policeman, I'm a landlord. John's a criminal. And it's us that suffer, not him.
I used to laugh when John said he was the true Prince of Wales. But now I think he's always believed it.
He's here isn't he, where is he?

HELEDD. I don't know, Sion.

SION. Where is he? I know you know where he is, where is he?

HELEDD. I don't know.

SION. I'll find him. I'll find him and when I do you'll never see him again.

HERBERT *enters* (*outside*), *in a bit of state.*

HERBERT. What, what is this? There's a policeman half dead. The convict's been back five minutes and this is what he drives you to? We are *civilised*.

SION. It was a misunderstanding.

HERBERT. A misunderstanding? If that's a misunderstanding with someone he calls a friend, what will the lout want to do with me? No, no, this cannot stand. He's been hiding in the shadows too long, we must flush him out.

SION. We'll find him.

HELEDD. You don't even know where he is.

HERBERT. In the shadows, lurking. With an assassin's grin. That man's had too many safe havens. We'll burn the shadows and we'll burn the havens

HELEDD. Well, he's not here so don't go burning the only pub for a mile.

HERBERT. No, he never is, is he? He's never anywhere. Well, he's not a necromancer, he's somewhere. And we will find him *tonight*. The police take an assault on one of their own very seriously. Every officer in North Wales is on his way to deal with this scoundrel.

If you ever wanted to rob a bank in Denbigh, tonight would be the night.

But there's little we can do if you continue to protect him.

SION. No one's protecting him.

HERBERT. No?

HELEDD. No.

HERBERT. I'll not be killed in my bed. I don't live in fear on my own land.

SION. He's got no friends here after what he's done to Eifion, trust me on that.

HERBERT. Well, the man who hands me John Jones will be rewarded, mark my words. Very well rewarded.

SION. I look forward to it.
I look forward to it.
If he turns up here Heledd, for God's sake do the decent thing. For Eifion if nothing else.

HELEDD. I hardly think he'll come here with everyone out looking for him.

HERBERT. Know how to handle a rifle, landlord?

SION. We're not shooting him.

HERBERT. I am.
You'd better find him first.

HERBERT *leaves* (*outside*).

HELEDD. Be careful, Sion.

SION. If I find you know where he's been hiding, I'll have your guts for garters, woman.

SION *leaves* (*outside*).

HELEDD. *Happy* now?
I know you're here.

COCH BACH *emerges from… somewhere.*

COCH BACH. I'm starting to go off the new boss.

HELEDD. I don't suppose he thinks much of you, either.

COCH BACH. What about you? You going off me too?

HELEDD. I could. Where's my ticket to the Dutch Antilles?

COCH BACH. Oh, there's no ticket. I said 'passage' to the Dutch Antilles. We'll *get* there.

HELEDD. Do you even know where the Dutch Antilles are?

COCH BACH. No idea. All I know is that they're nowhere near Holland and that's fine by me.
Heledd, I need you to get me some things.

HELEDD. Like what?

COCH BACH. Herbs, plants, roots, anything like that. A selection.

HELEDD. Do you want to be a bit more specific?

COCH BACH. It doesn't matter, I just need a variety. Picked wild.
And Tomos. I need your Tomos.

HELEDD. Right. Going to tell me why?

COCH BACH. No.

HELEDD. And what are you going to do?

COCH BACH. I need to have a chat with someone.

HELEDD. The Dutch Antilles better be *brilliant*.

COCH BACH. You'll make someone a lovely wife one day, Heledd

HELEDD *glares. A warning.*

HELEDD *leaves (outside).*

COCH BACH *hears footsteps from outside and hides.*

JOHN JNR *enters (outside).*

JOHN JNR. Heledd? Sion?

COCH BACH *comes out.*

COCH BACH. Psst.

JOHN JNR. Dad!

COCH BACH. Shh. That's it, let everyone know I'm here.

JOHN JNR. Sorry. You're back…

COCH BACH. Think your old dad was going to abandon you after all these years?

JOHN JNR. Well. Yeah.

COCH BACH. Alright, I deserved that. Not been the best father I suppose, have I?

JOHN JNR. It's been hard to tell.

COCH BACH. Aye. What are you now, seventeen?

JOHN JNR. Nineteen.

COCH BACH. Oh. Not filled out much have you? Look at that chest. I've seen more meat on a pigeon.

JOHN JNR. I'm still growing.

COCH BACH. I wouldn't bet on it, youth. We've never been a tall lot.
My son and heir. There he is.
Well. Here I am.
It was good to see you again.
Take me in then. You got me.

JOHN JNR. What?

COCH BACH. Take me in, hand me over.
That's what you wanted to do, isn't it? Hand me over, get the reward.

JOHN JNR. I don't want the reward.

COCH BACH. I'm not talking about the money, boy.
Come on, else Sion'll be here in a minute and he'll steal your glory.

JOHN JNR. I don't know what you're talking about.

COCH BACH. Aye, you do.
I often wondered whether you were my son. Your mother, she was
Let's just say I wondered.
But here the other night, in front of that beautiful girl. You proved you were the son of John Jones of Bala. We've a proud line in selling out our own fathers.

JOHN JNR. I wasn't. I wasn't going to. Where'd you

COCH BACH. She's beautiful, eh.

JOHN JNR. Yeah. But. You're my father.

COCH BACH. No, I'm not. Not really. Not in there I'm not. I might have given your mother one but then a lot of lads did. Sion's been more of a father to you than I have.

JOHN JNR. Listen, yeah, I was thinking about it, alright, I was. Beatrice wanted me to, she thought it would make her father, I don't know, grateful or something

COCH BACH. I know. Grand idea.

JOHN JNR. But after what's happened to Eifion, they're talking about hanging you. Hanging you, Dad.

COCH BACH. Maybe I *should* hang.

JOHN JNR. I'm not letting that happen. I should never have told Beatrice that I would. I'll help you get away, somewhere anywhere. I could join up with you later. There's such a fuss outside we could sneak away easy.

COCH BACH. You'd choose me over her?

JOHN JNR. Yes.

COCH BACH. I wouldn't. Trust me, I wouldn't.

JOHN JNR. I don't know what I was thinking. You're my father. I've been
I've always been proud of you, proud to be your son.
I have, I have.
I've waited, I've been waiting for you. To come back.
And as soon as you do I think about selling you out for some girl.

COCH BACH. Proud of me? Proud of what?

JOHN JNR. You're a legend. Proud of, what you've done.

COCH BACH. What have I done?

JOHN JNR. You've. Well.

    1871, you scale the wall of Ruthin Gaol, twenty foot high, whilst the jailers were exchanging keys. Incredible.

    1873, you steal the grand piano from

COCH BACH. No.

JOHN JNR. 1882, you escape from Stafford Gaol by tunneling through the cell wall. With a cake fork.

    1885, you steal the Sheriff of Chester's hat and hide it

COCH BACH. No. It's all lies, boy. I made it all up. You think I have honour? There's no honour here. I steal and I rob. And I go to jail. Sometimes I tell a tall story for a bowl of soup and roof over my head.

JOHN JNR. No, no. You're *famous*. You're the Welsh Houdini. You're a hero. You were in the papers.

COCH BACH. I am a crook. Nothing else.

JOHN JNR. Everyone says it. Everyone tells the stories, not just you. I've had a hundred different people tell me about you. And they *love* you.

COCH BACH. *Lies*. I'm a good thief but I'm a bloody wonderful liar.

    I've spent more time in jail than out of it. And last time round they should have locked me up and thrown away the key. For what I done.

JOHN JNR. You done nothing.

COCH BACH. No?

JOHN JNR. No. You said so yourself. I heard you. It was ridiculous what they said. Beating an old woman like that, for five pounds. You've stolen things worth a hundred times that without so much as turning over a leaf. Beating an old woman to a pulp, for five pounds? Someone did that but not you. Not Coch Bach y Bala. Not my father. I know it.

    You said it yourself. Why would you do something so horrific for five pounds?

COCH BACH. BECAUSE I WANTED FIVE POUNDS.

I wanted it. She had it. I took it.

Know why I beat her so hard?

Because she didn't want me to have it. And then I beat her again in case she had five pounds more I didn't know about. Died, didn't she? Few months later.

Know what I spent the five pounds on?

Nor do I. Can't remember.

JOHN JNR.

COCH BACH. Want me to be a part of your life, do you? I don't.

I'm off.

Soon as I've had my fun here, I was going to be off.

I've got a son like you in every bloody town.

So

If I do one decent thing in my life. It's this.

We'll make it look like I struggled. Herbert *will* be grateful. Take me in.

Take me in, John.

Take me in, son.

She's *beautiful*.

Take me in. Boy.

That's a better life than I can give you.

Please.

Please, take me in, son.

JOHN JNR *leaves* (*outside*).

COCH BACH *finds something – chalk? – and draws a circle around the cauldron.*

COCH BACH *stands on the bar/a table, over the cauldron. He takes a knife and cuts his palm. He squeezes the blood into it.*

(*To the air.*) Well, why not now?

COCH BACH *opens the front door.*

COME QUICK
COME QUICK

I HAVE HIM. I HAVE COCH BACH Y BALA
COME
HE'S HERE THE CONVICT IS IN HERE

COCH BACH *steps into the circle by the cauldron.*

SION *enters (outside).*

Thank goodness you came!

SION. What are you doing?

COCH BACH. He was just here. He went that way, quick!

SION. Who?

COCH BACH. Coch Bach y Bala. The notorious criminal. He's getting away!

SION. What are you doing?

COCH BACH. What are *you* doing?

SION. HE'S HERE, HE'S IN HERE. COCH BACH IS HERE.

SION *goes at* COCH BACH.

COCH BACH. Ah ah ah! I wouldn't do that.

COCH BACH *points to the circle.* SION *stops.*

That's it, no further. You don't want to be in here with me.

SION. Coch, there's police everywhere. There's nowhere to go.

COCH BACH. And that's fine. But you know me well enough to just stay where you are for now.

HELEDD *enters (outside) with a sack containing the flowers, herbs, etc…*

HELEDD. Sion. You caught him.

COCH BACH. Oh no no.

SION. You don't catch Coch.

COCH BACH. I'm handing myself in. Peacefully.

SION. Come on then.

COCH BACH. Something I need to do first.
  Thanks, Heledd. Where's Tomos?

HELEDD. He's coming.

SION. Tomos?

  HELEDD *passes the sack to* COCH BACH.

  What's in there?

HELEDD. Leaves mainly.

SION. What for?

HELEDD. Ask him.

COCH BACH. You'll see.

  TOMOS *and* JOHN JNR *enter* (*outside*).

TOMOS. Coch!

JOHN JNR. What's happening?

SION. He's turning himself in.

JOHN JNR. No, Dad. No! Why?

  TOMOS *and* JOHN JNR *move to one side of the pub,
  making a natural divide between them and* SION, COCH
  BACH *and* HELEDD.

TOMOS. What are you doing, Coch? Why you drawn on the
  floor?

COCH BACH. Just trying to help.

  HERBERT *enters* (*outside*).

HERBERT. We have him? We have him!

  SION *uses this moment to rush* COCH BACH *and pins him.*

  Seize the brute, well done that man!

JOHN JNR. Whose side are you *on*, Sion? That's Coch Bach y
  Bala.

COCH BACH. You shouldn't have come inside the circle, Sion.

SION. I know exactly who he is, thank you, I've had a lifetime of him.

HERBERT. Good man.

JOHN JNR. You're not handing him over.

COCH BACH. That was a mistake, Sion.

SION. He had his chance, John. He left. And now he's back. And this is the price he pays. He's dragging us all through the muck.

TOMOS. Who's side are *you* on, Mam?

HELEDD. Be quiet, Tomos.

SION. Look what's happened to Eifion. I'm sorry, John. I am, I am sorry to say it. But this is what happens when your father is around.

JOHN JNR. This isn't up to you, Sion.

SION. I love him with all my soul but I swear to God I won't go to prison just so's he can fuck about.
We can't *have* him here.

COCH BACH. Listen to him, son. I'm a devil, you need shot of me.

JOHN JNR. What are you going to do with him?

HERBERT. Send him back to prison. What else would you do with an escaped convict? He'll be lucky to escape the noose this time.

JOHN JNR. I wasn't talking to you.
Let him go, Sion. You can't do it, you're outnumbered.

SION. No I'm not.

TOMOS. You are if I join John's side.

SION. We're not going to have a *fight,* Tom.

JOHN JNR. Let my father go, Sion, and you're right.
What you doing, Sion?

HERBERT. Sion has proved a decent man and he's getting rid

JOHN JNR. I'm not *talking to you.*
 Sion?

SION. Enough's enough, John. He's a liability. The rest of you
 might want to stand by as he plays merry hell but I can't.

TOMOS. John, I'm not sure if I'm going to join your side or
 not, sorry.

SION. This isn't cowboys and Indians, Tomos.

JOHN JNR. Can everyone just work out whose side they're on?
 Heledd?

TOMOS. If I'm with you, John, it's three against one. Are we
 counting Herbert?

SION. Two against two, Coch can't move.

TOMOS. Nor can you if you're holding him, so it's actually
 two against none.

SION. What?

JOHN JNR. He's right. Unless Herbert fancies it.

HERBERT. I'm having nothing to do with this.

SION. Heledd can scrap. Where do you stand, love?

HELEDD. Behind the bar.

TOMOS. I think I might be neutral, John.

JOHN JNR. And see my dad hanged?

TOMOS. Yeah.
 No!

COCH BACH. Can I intervene?

SION. Why not, eh? You don't usually ask.

COCH BACH (*to* JOHN JNR *and* TOMOS). Boys, I've been
 caught. Bang to rights. Let it go. Reginald'll be here soon to
 cart me off. I'm not resisting. Fair's fair, it's done.

JOHN JNR. It doesn't have to be, Dad.

TOMOS. I think we still outnumber them, Coch. I think.

COCH BACH. Them? Who's them?

TOMOS. My dad. And

COCH BACH. Your *dad*?

TOMOS. Yeah but he's your mate and look at him.

COCH BACH. Aye, but I done wrong, Tomos. Get that through your thick head. I've broken the law. Your dad's just doing his bit.

JOHN JNR. Dad, there's still a chance before the police come.

COCH BACH. Be quiet, boy. A man knows when to fight and when not to.

TOMOS. Do we fight now? Cos we could.

COCH BACH. That it, Tom? Got fight in you?

TOMOS. I think so.

COCH BACH. Think so, eh?

REGINALD *enters (outside), with rifle.*

REGINALD. Thank goodness. Well done, Sion.

HERBERT. Where are the police?

REGINALD. Outside. I told them I'd bring him out.

COCH BACH. Let us go, Sion. You must be awful sore standing there like that.

REGINALD. I have him, Sion. You can let him go.

REGINALD *trains the rifle on* COCH BACH. SION *lets* COCH BACH *go.*

COCH BACH. Thank you, Sion.
I'm not resisting, Reginald. But I do ask for a minute. One minute? To talk to my friends?
Next spell in prison's my last, eh?

REGINALD. I wouldn't worry. I told the police to enter in five
     minutes anyway.
     You're cornered.

COCH BACH. I know.
     I just wanted a moment to talk to young Tom, here.

TOM. Me?

COCH BACH. Yeah, you.
     What do you all think of my cauldron?
     Big, eh?
     Did Heledd tell you where I got it?

SION. Heledd said she hadn't seen you.

COCH BACH. Know why I came back, Tom? I coulda just run.
     But I came back.

TOMOS. I don't know why you went.

COCH BACH. I went to get this, Tom. And I came back
     because I need to tell you one or two things.
     One, before this is all out I am going to die. And, Tom,
     because you are a soldier, I can trust you with this and I want
     you to promise me something…

TOMOS. Promise you what?

COCH BACH. After I die I want you to remove my head from
     my shoulders. And I want you to carry it with you. And
     never fear, I'll still be good company. Your regiment will
     like me. I know all the songs and all the bawdy jokes. You'll
     carry me and you'll carry me and eventually you'll bury
     me in Italy, on the banks of the Natisone, alongside my pal
     Magnus Maximus. Bear in mind I'm facing home, young
     Tom.
     I will miss it.

TOMOS. Alright…

REGINALD. Is this how you do it? Fill children's minds with
     mumbo jumbo? So they think you're some kind of mystic?

COCH BACH. I don't want you to be afraid, Tom.

TOMOS. I won't.

COCH BACH. Yes, you will. But I don't want you to be.
   Remember that.
   No matter how afraid or how alone you are, there's someone
   out there that wishes you weren't.
   I went to Ireland to get this.
   Because people are going to die. Because people are going to
   die and I don't know what else I can do.

HERBERT. Is he always this theatrical?

COCH BACH. And men like Herbert, Tom. Will always be
   there to put you down. Men like Herbert will never die.

REGINALD. Jones, I know what you're doing. You're using
   these people as a distraction and I see right through you. Out.
   (*To* TOMOS *and* JOHN JNR.) You two. Let's get this over
   with.

TOMOS. Why me?

REGINALD. John Jones is going back to prison. Would you
   like to join him?

JOHN JNR. Come on, Tomos. He's turning himself in anyway.

REGINALD. Thank you.

TOMOS. What does the cauldron do, Coch?

COCH BACH. Nothing. S'just a story.

TOMOS. What story?

   TOMOS *and* JOHN JNR *leave* (*outside*).

REGINALD. Landlord, please escort your wife and my father
   out.
   All John Jones wants is an audience, I'm afraid we'll have to
   deprive him of one.

HERBERT. Careful.

REGINALD. Thank you. I am being.

HERBERT. I should stay.

REGINALD. He wants you here.

HELEDD, SION and HERBERT leave (outside).

Now. Are you going to come or shall bring in the police?

COCH BACH. Do you want to know why I brought the cauldron in?

REGINALD. No.
Yes.

COCH BACH. Legend has it
That's always a bad start that
But. Legend has it, we gave this cauldron to the Irish as a gift. Hundreds of years ago. The story goes that they would put the bodies of young dead soldiers, who'd been slain in battle, into the cauldron. And the next morning they would be alive. Their voices taken from them as payment.

REGINALD. And you believe that?

COCH BACH. Yes.
One thing. One thing?

COCH BACH stands on the table, with the sack. One by one he takes out the contents of the sack, rejecting some, but breaking and sprinkling others into the cauldron. Again he takes a knife, and cuts his other palm, letting the blood run into the cauldron.

That's it. That's all.

*COCH BACH comes down and leaves (outside),
REGINALD follows him.*

Outside we can hear COCH BACH arrested by the police.

A moment before...

TOMOS enters, sneaking in.

He goes to the cauldron and looks inside.

He gasps.

End of Act Two.

ACT THREE

The Death of Coch Bach y Bala

October sixth, eleven-thirty p.m. Monday.

The White Horse.

The cauldron has gone.

Alone, in semi-darkness, a patched up WINSTANLEY *sits, drinking. He is still covered in cuts, bruises, etc.*

He drinks.

He briefly sings 'Hen Ferchetan'.

WINSTANLEY. Hen ferchetan wedi colli'i chariad
Ffol-di rol-di rol-lol ffol-di rol-di ro

He drinks.

HELEDD *enters (inside).*

HELEDD. Still here, Constable?

WINSTANLEY. Oh I'm not going anywhere.

HELEDD. Would you like the spare bed again?

WINSTANLEY. That would be best. Thank you, Heledd.

HELEDD. It's no problem. It's nice to have some company.

WINSTANLEY. He'll be back. I know Sion. It won't be you
he's cross with, he'll probably never forgive himself for
turning on Coch.
But it had to be done.
He'll just need some thinking time. Some drinking time.

HELEDD. Aye, well. Even if he comes back he'll have no one
to serve in this place.

An urgent knock at the front door.

We're closed.

Another urgent knock.

Fine, fine. We need the custom.

HELEDD *goes to the door.*

WINSTANLEY. Careful. It could be… anyone.

HELEDD *unbolts and opens the door.*

HELEDD. Oh. Hello.

REGINALD *enters (outside), slightly frantic.*

REGINALD. Is she here?

HELEDD. Is who here?

REGINALD. Beatrice. Is she here?

HELEDD. No one but me and the Constable, why?

REGINALD. Then where is she?

WINSTANLEY. She gone, has she?

REGINALD. We thought she was in her room. She's spent almost every waking hour in her room the last few days, so we didn't think to look. But Francis went in now and she's gone.

WINSTANLEY. Where might she go?

REGINALD. I have no idea.
I think she's been taken.
This is revenge, I tell you. That's what this is, revenge.

HELEDD. Is young John Jones home?

REGINALD. Why?

HELEDD. You might want to check.

REGINALD. What would he have done with her?

WINSTANLEY. I'll go see.

REGINALD. What would John have done? What would they want with her?

WINSTANLEY. I shall return shortly.

REGINALD. I'll come with you.

WINSTANLEY. No, no. I won't be a moment. He's only across the way.

WINSTANLEY *leaves* (*outside*).

HELEDD. Sit down, love.

REGINALD *sits.*

You need to get thoughts of John Jones, John Jones senior that is, out of your mind

REGINALD. How can I?

HELEDD. At least as far as Beatrice is concerned.

REGINALD. My sister

HELEDD. is probably with young John.

REGINALD. Where would he have taken her?

HELEDD. I don't think he would have *taken* her. She'd have gone happily.

REGINALD. Why?

HELEDD. If she's with John, she'll be safe. Don't worry.

REGINALD. Why didn't I know about this?

HELEDD. I don't think you were meant to.

REGINALD. Beatrice?

HELEDD. Young love, eh?

REGINALD. They've eloped?

HELEDD. That would be my guess, yes.

WINSTANLEY *enters* (*outside*).

REGINALD. Well?

WINSTANLEY. Gone. Drawers empty and all.

REGINALD. I don't believe this. Constable, I would like you to treat this as a kidnapping.

WINSTANLEY. Well we hardly know

HELEDD. She's gone with open arms and open eyes, trust me.

REGINALD. My sister would never have anything to do with
any of you.
Constable, start the search. How far could they have got?

WINSTANLEY. Apologies, but I am off duty.
For reasons I hardly need to go into.

REGINALD. Then what are you doing here?

WINSTANLEY. Drinking. You'd be amazed what a bit of
whisky does for cracked ribs.

HELEDD. For all you know they've been planning this for
weeks. They could be on a boat to America by now.

REGINALD. My father. Is in tears. I promised him I would not
return without her.

WINSTANLEY. Well, that could be a while. Why don't you
wait in here with me? Have a drink

REGINALD. With you? What, while you wait for a ghost to
turn up?

WINSTANLEY. He's coming. Don't you worry.

REGINALD. He's dead, Constable. John Jones is dead.
This is why his son has kidnapped my sister. As revenge
because he holds us responsible. And I would appreciate you
doing your duty as a police officer and helping me apprehend
a criminal.

WINSTANLEY. No.

REGINALD. He's *not coming*. He was shot twice during his
escape and fell twenty foot from the prison wall. The last
scrap of clothing he had was found washed up by the river.

Your faith in him is infantile. It is below zero out there and
he was naked and wounded. That was four days ago. The
man is dead. He has drowned.

WINSTANLEY. He's had worse.

REGINALD. What do I tell my father?

HELEDD. Why don't you get some sleep? There's nothing you can do tonight.

REGINALD. What, so he can get halfway across the country with her? Or does whatever he's planning to do to her? Look at his father, men like him are savages. I'll not leave my poor sister with him a minute longer than I have to.
Where would they have gone?

HELEDD. Gretna Green?

REGINALD. Before John Jones returned, you all did such a good job of pretending to be civilised.

REGINALD leaves (outside).

WINSTANLEY. If Coch comes, he'll wake you. Wake me too, please Heledd.

I don't mean him any harm.

WINSTANLEY leaves (inside).

HELEDD (*to the birds*). You not seen him, have you?
Thought not.

HELEDD locks the front door and leaves (inside).

A moment.

Noise. Someone breaking in. Quietly. Carefully.

In comes COCH BACH.

He is a state. His nakedness covered only by a sack which he has fashioned into a kind of smock. He is soaked through, wild-eyed and feral. He limps, his back and left shoulder bleed, he is pale and shaking. He is barely conscious and weak as a rag doll.

He looks around, quietly, careful not to disturb anyone.

He holds in a howl as he warms himself by the fire.

*He reaches inside his smock/sack and pulls out a bag, which
he has clearly stolen. He sits on the floor and pulls out its
contents, also stolen, to inspect them.*

Three tallow candles – he is unimpressed.

A garden gnome – he chuckles.

*A half empty bottle of methylated spirits – he takes a large
swig.*

A trowel – he weighs it up and arms himself with it.

And waits.

And gets bored.

And takes a swig of meths.

And stands up.

And knocks something over, making a racket.

*He returns to his slumped position on the floor, armed with
the trowel.*

HELEDD *enters* (*inside*).

Hello? Hello, who's there?

She spots COCH BACH.

John!

COCH BACH. Hello
    Lovely.

HELEDD. Oh my God, John. Are you alright?

COCH BACH. Just
    Dandy. Never
    Been better.

HELEDD. Are you hurt?

COCH BACH. Nah.

HELEDD. You're freezing.

COCH BACH. *Hungry.*

HELEDD. Constable! Eifion!
  Eifion, come quick.

COCH BACH. Food
  Please.

HELEDD. Hang on, John. We need to get you warm.
  You're bleeding!

COCH BACH. Scratch
  S'all.

  WINSTANLEY *enters* (*inside*).

WINSTANLEY. Heledd?
  Well, well, well
  It's King Arthur.

HELEDD. Eifion, go upstairs, get blankets, a shirt, trousers,
  anything. Keep him warm. I'm going to get a doctor. Just
  keep him warm for now.

WINSTANLEY. No problem.

HELEDD. John, love. I won't be long. I'm going to get the
  doctor.
  Come on, Eifion. Hurry.

  HELEDD *unlocks the door and leaves* (*outside*).

WINSTANLEY. You look like I felt a few days ago.

  Looks at Coch's possessions.

  What you got here?
  Who's this?

  Picks up the gnome.

  Hello. That's nice that is.
  Candles there too.
  What's this? Meths, is it?

  COCH BACH *nods*.

  Want some?

COCH BACH *nods.*

WINSTANLEY *uncaps the bottle and gives it to* COCH BACH *who drinks.*

There we are.
And this? A *trowel.* Going to do some gardening, were you?

COCH BACH. Food
'm starvin

WINSTANLEY. I got no food, no.
I knew you'd be back. You always have to come back, don't you?
Do they even put locks on prison doors, these days?
Eh? Too clever by half, you are.

COCH BACH. Eifion
I'm sorry.

WINSTANLEY. Sure.
Let's have a look at you. A look at your face.

COCH BACH. Some bread
Eifion
Please

WINSTANLEY *spits in* COCH BACH*'s face.*

WINSTANLEY. Piss off. Convict.

WINSTANLEY *leaves (outside).*

COCH BACH *looks around.*

He picks up one of the tallow candles. Eats it.

REGINALD *enters (outside), with rifle.*

REGINALD. Constable? Constable, my father would like you to

Good God.

COCH BACH *waggles the trowel.*

COCH BACH. Don't
Take 'nother step

REGINALD. You're not dead.

COCH BACH *drops the trowel.*

COCH BACH. 'm I not?

REGINALD. Don't move.

COCH BACH. Fine.

REGINALD. Where is my sister?

COCH BACH. Ah. Lovely Beatrice
What a
Beautif–

REGINALD. Where is she?

COCH BACH *struggles to his feet, he slaps himself awake.*

Where is my sister?

COCH BACH. Where's my badger?

REGINALD. Dead. I shot it.

COCH BACH. No…

REGINALD. You had poor Tom fooled alright. We kept telling him the badger was clearly never dead in the first place. But your magic still works on simpletons.

COCH BACH. They did a favour for me.

REGINALD. And we had a hell of a time explaining to the owners of Bodidris Hall how their ornamental cauldron had ended up in a pub three miles down the road.

COCH BACH. You never get bored of pointin' a gun at me?

REGINALD. *Yes.*
Your son has kidnapped my sister. Where has he taken her?

COCH BACH. He's…?

REGINALD. Both of them are missing. I hardly think Beatrice would have gone with him willingly. John was desperate after he thought you'd died. This is revenge against my father and me. A pathetic game.

COCH BACH. Your sister will bear my grandchildren.
Gladly.

REGINALD *hits* COCH BACH *with the butt of his rifle.*
COCH BACH *slumps again.*

REGINALD. You're not going to prison this time. Iron bars
seem to have little effect on you.
But before I put you out of your misery, you're going to tell
me where your son has taken Beatrice.

COCH BACH. I know a place.
South of here

REGINALD. Yes?

COCH BACH. In the Berwyns, the mountains

REGINALD. Yes? Whereabouts?

COCH BACH. A mile or two northwest of Llanrhaeadr ym
Mochnant
Near the summit of Moel Sych

REGINALD. Yes? And what's there?

COCH BACH. Pistyll Rhaeadr
S'a waterfall
S'beautiful, you really should see it. Whilst you're here.

REGINALD. And they've gone there?

COCH BACH. Who now?

REGINALD. Beatrice and
I am trying to help you.

COCH BACH. Huzzah.

REGINALD. If we find Beatrice, unharmed. *Soon.*
Then we will be lenient on John. If you can help us find him.
Your dying breath could save your son's life. After a lifetime
of wasting it, why not?
The fact that I don't know where Beatrice is is the only
reason I haven't shot you yet.

COCH BACH. Why are you so scared of me?

REGINALD. I am not scared of you but you are a threat.

COCH BACH. A threat? But you, are the invader. On my land.

REGINALD. Land we bought.

COCH BACH. From me?

REGINALD. It wasn't yours to sell.

COCH BACH. It wasn't anyone's to sell.
   If I was to round up fifty of the heartiest lads and storm
   Eyarth Hall when you slept in your beds, would you fall at
   our feet? Would make yourself our slave?
   Or would you fight tooth and nail? Would you rather die,
   than see your home fall into the hands of strangers? Would
   you risk oblivion over servitude? Of course you would.
   Don't hate me for doing what you would do.
   Shoot me. But don't hate me.
   I came back to protect people from *you*.

REGINALD. I am not a villain
   I am trying to do my best. It is you that won't let us live in
   peace.

COCH BACH. That's right. I won't.
   Not whilst you and your family roost upon my land. Not
   whilst you and your father claim ownership over my land.

REGINALD. I've heard quite enough. Where are they?

COCH BACH. I don't know.

REGINALD. Where are they?

COCH BACH. The badger was dead.

REGINALD. Where has he taken her?

COCH BACH. Kill me and you kill a king.
   You know what happens when you kill a king?

REGINALD. I'm not playing games.

COCH BACH. Kill me and you'll be haunted forever.
   Kill me and you'll bring Bendigeidfran after you.
   Kill me and Arawn king of Annwn will drag his hounds of
   war over you and the people you care about.

REGINALD. Save your nonsense

COCH BACH. Beli Mawr, Pwyll Prince of Dyfed.
The Silures, the Demetae, the Deceangli, the Ordovices.
Caradog, Cynddylan, Rhodri Mawr, Gruffudd ap Llewelyn.
What did you pay any of them?

REGINALD. Nothing. They got nothing. And you'll get
nothing.
Anything else?

COCH BACH. Shhh.

REGINALD. Last chance, Jones. Where's your son?

COCH BACH. Shhhh.

REGINALD. Fine. I gave you a chance

COCH BACH. *Shhhh.*

REGINALD. What?

COCH BACH. Sing.

REGINALD. Wh–

COCH BACH. *Sing.*

The birds sing.

REGINALD. How are you doing

COCH BACH. Shhhh

The birds sing.

REGINALD. How are you

COCH BACH. You are not your father.
Reginald Jones-Bateman
I don't think you're a bad man.

The birds sing.

REGINALD. How are you doing it?

COCH BACH. Shhh. It's alright.

REGINALD. How did you escape Ruthin Gaol? They told me
they had a dozen men guarding you.

COCH BACH. Two dozen.

REGINALD. I don't know what to do.

In my worst nightmares, the world is filled with men like
you. Men that won't be told.
I can't kill you all.

REGINALD *slumps down by* COCH BACH.

Does your son love Beatrice?

COCH BACH. He's a good one, that boy.

REGINALD. He'll take care of her?

COCH BACH. Like a princess.

REGINALD. You really stink.

COCH BACH. Oh, aye.

REGINALD. Do you know I've never lived in England?
Everyone round here calls me English – *Saes* – but I've spent
about two weeks there in my life.

COCH BACH. You should try it. Nice place. Food's a bit iffy.

REGINALD. You were shot. At the prison.

REGINALD *inspects* COCH BACH.

Magician or not, those wounds need tending to.
I'll get help.
Here.

REGINALD *takes off his coat and helps* COCH BACH *into
it.*

COCH BACH. Heledd's gone.

REGINALD. My mother was a nurse. I'll get her. She could be
here in minutes.
Stay here.

COCH BACH. Yeah, why not? I'm comfy.

REGINALD. I don't know what we're going to do. Coch Bach. I don't know what to do.

REGINALD *leaves* (*outside*).

A moment.

FRANCIS *enters* (*outside*), *with a double-barrelled shotgun. He checks* REGINALD *has definitely gone before closing the door.* COCH BACH *struggles to his feet.*

COCH BACH. Now here's the real feast.

FRANCIS *shoots* COCH BACH. *Despite the obvious force of the shot,* COCH BACH *remains standing.*

FRANCIS. How did you make the birds sing?

COCH BACH. Ah…

FRANCIS. How did you make the birds sing?

COCH BACH. How do you think?

FRANCIS. How did you do it? I demand to know.

COCH BACH. What about *your* nightmares, Francis? What are they filled with?

FRANCIS. I don't have nightmares.

COCH BACH. You will.

COCH BACH *throws the gnome at* FRANCIS.

FRANCIS *shoots* COCH BACH *again.*

COCH BACH *falls.*

C'mere

FRANCIS. Why?

COCH BACH. C'mere

FRANCIS *goes to* COCH BACH.

COCH BACH *reaches into this sack and pulls something out. He dangles it on his fingers.* FRANCIS*'s locket.* FRANCIS *gasps and checks his neck.*

FRANCIS. My locket!

FRANCIS *grabs the locket.*

How did you get it?

COCH BACH *laughs.*

How did you get it?

COCH BACH *grabs* FRANCIS *by the collar and pulls them face to face.*

COCH BACH. Magic.

COCH BACH *dies.*

REGINALD *enters* (*outside*).

REGINALD. Francis, what have you done?

FRANCIS. How did he make the birds sing?

HELEDD *enters* (*outside*).

HELEDD. Mr Jone–
Francis
What are you

HELEDD *sees* COCH BACH.

Oh no

HELEDD *goes to* COCH BACH.

No

REGINALD. I had no choice.
I'm sorry.
He attacked me.

HELEDD. Attacked you? He could barely stand.

REGINALD. He is *dangerous*, what was I supposed to do? He came at me. Look at the mess here. He was wild.
He gave me no choice, I was afraid for my life. I'm sorry.

HELEDD. Get out.

REGINALD. I didn't want this.

HELEDD. Please.

REGINALD. If he'd just have
    If he'd have given us a *chance.*
    Come, Francis.

HELEDD. This will follow you.
    Third Battalion, isn't it? Royal Welsh.
    Enjoy your war, Reginald.

    REGINALD *and* FRANCIS *leave* (*outside*).

    HELEDD *holds* COCH BACH.

    The birds sing.

    The End.

Acknowledgements

I would like to thank all those who have, each in their own way, been instrumental in developing this play. Namely, John Ginman, Erica Davies, Al Smith, Stewart Pringle, James Graham, Richard Alford, Gareth Jandrell, John Jones, everyone at Theatr Clwyd, Dan Jones and the cast, my parents, and Bekah. But most of all Kate Wasserberg, who kept the faith.

C.A-B.